PRESIDENTIAL AND CAMPAIGN MEMORABILIA

WITH PRICES

SECOND EDITION

STAN GORES

On the front cover
    Rarely found anywhere outside the Smithsonian Institution, this dramatic McKinley campaign poster from 1900 shows the President holding the flag, smiling, and doffing his hat while standing atop a gold coin labeled "Sound Money." The coin is held aloft by workmen and aristocrats alike, along with servicemen and a Civil War veteran who holds high his blue hat marked "GAR." All are rejoicing at the newfound Prosperity under the McKinley administration. In the background are two secondary themes, Commerce and Civilization. Old sailing ships can be seen at the dock, with barrels stacked on shore and horse-pulled wagons on the scene. The other side of the poster pictures smoke from busy factories and a freight train pulling into the dock area. Framed, the rare poster is nearly 29″ wide × 43″ high. **$1,000**

On the backcover
    This 1900 poster for McKinley's reelection is one of the most glamorized campaign posters of all time. It has a handsome jugate display of McKinley and Roosevelt beneath two American flags under a heading, "The Administration's Promises Have Been Kept." Three scenes on each side of the poster contrast life in 1896, when McKinley took over, and in 1900, after he'd been in the White House for four years. Reversed in that time, according to the theme, were both an economy that saw factories standing idle and banks in trouble and Spanish rule in Cuba. Also included is McKinley's disclaimer that "The American Flag has not been planted in foreign soil to acquire more territory, but for Humanity's sake." Great graphics. 16¾″ × 24⅝″, framed. **$550**

Cover design and interior layout: Anthony Jacobson
Photography: Ted Kremer
Editor: Stephen Levy

Library of Congress Catalog Card Number 87-51677

ISBN 0-87069-516-9

Copyright 1988, Wallace-Homestead Book Company
All rights reserved.

10 9 8 7 6 5 4 3 2 1

Published by

A Capital Cities/ABC, Inc. Company

Wallace-Homestead Book Company
Post Office Box 5406
Greensboro, NC 27403
(919) 275-9809

Contents

To the family

Foreword

Over the years, collecting has steadily gained popularity. In this time of unprecedented growth in collecting, today's collectors enjoy all the advantages that were missing in the past.

There are abundant sources for finding collectibles—antique shows, specialized collector meetings and flea markets of record size. There are local and national collector organizations. And there are valuable reference materials—like this book.

Collecting American political memorabilia, the subject of this book, is especially rewarding. Like many other collectors, those who collect political items have the luxury of a national organization; it's known as the American Political Items Collectors. But there's more. Political items have a special appeal. They are uniquely American and historically significant. They mirror the social and political climate in this country, from its fledgling days as a new democracy to the present.

In addition, they reflect the progression of American technology and ingenuity. The types of items issued during campaigns have evolved from primitive brass clothing buttons to sophisticated plastic buttons that play music and feature flashing lights. No other hobby so deeply traces the history and technology of our country.

We are indeed lucky to be collecting today. Advanced technology has made fascinating and unique political items available to add to our collections. The items we seek are easier than ever to locate and are becoming increasingly more interesting. Plus, we have the added bonus of this book which offers a ready source of information to the collector and provides the knowledge and expertise required to have a successful collection experience.

Geary Vlk
President
American Political Items Collectors

For information about APIC, write:
American Political Items Collectors
P.O. Box 340339
San Antonio, TX 78234-0339

Acknowledgments

Expanding the size and content of *Presidential and Campaign Memorabilia* for this second edition has required the assistance and participation of many.

It has meant taking the first book and building on it—adding much new information, inserting current prices, and picturing more collectible items of all descriptions and value. Most notable has been the inclusion of more political buttons and their sometimes startling prices.

Assembling such a comprehensive edition has taken months of planning, historical research, contacts with collectors and knowledgeable sellers, trips to antique shows and flea markets—plus long hours of writing and organizing to pull it all together.

But, from beginning to end, once again I have been impressed by the kindness of all those who have joined me to make their personal contributions. It started when William N. Topaz, General Manager of Wallace-Homestead Books, gave his enthusiastic go-ahead; and it continued as Stephen Levy, Editor of Wallace-Homestead, began setting the editorial guidelines.

In mentioning names for this comprehensive second edition, I again pay deserved tribute to photographer Ted Kremer. After working with Ted on three books, I am more impressed than ever at the way he consistently manages to combine artistic photographic quality with that elusive necessity called speed. He is one of those rare individuals who always does more than asked—and makes working a pleasure.

The same is true of Tom Kitchen, a collector-friend of many years who agreed to disassemble his whole button collection for picture-taking, and who also handled the organizational chore of preparing the button pages for insertion in the book on the basis of presidential elections from 1896 through 1984. Not only that, but he tackled the job of seeing to it that the buttons were reasonably priced and in line with current markets. His personal interest, his conscientious follow-through and attention to detail are deeply appreciated in the production of this edition.

Special thanks are due Joe Brown, who again provided access to his remarkable political collection, thereby enabling us to fill-in on the scarcity button years and other collecting areas as well. While ranking among the top collectors in the nation, Joe also remains dedicated to helping promote the hobby among beginners and experienced collectors alike.

Speaking of leaders in the hobby, many others have made important contributions to the book. Geary Vlk, President of the American Political Items Collectors, has written a foreword in which he notes that mementos from our presidents "mirror the social and political climate in this country." Certainly a study of American campaign buttons and their slogans would support that observation.

On the always sensitive matter of pricing, assistance has been graciously given by some of the top experts in the field—Al Anderson, David Frent, Rex Stark, Kurt Krueger and Charles McSorley. Individuals with special collections, knowledge, or skills—such as John Henigan, Darlene and Jeff Schultz, John Reiland and Larry Bower—also have responded in ways that merit heartfelt gratitude.

But in discussing this expanded edition, I am not forgetting others who played such helpful roles in putting together the first edition in 1982—Jack Putman, a friend and collector of long experience; Herbert Collins of the Smithsonian Institution; Gene McLane, a family friend and library director with a keen sense of history; Sharon Albright, a good friend and antique dealer; and Blaine Hedberg, a genealogist who has an eye for the interesting and the unique.

And last, there's my wife, Jeannine, and the whole family—to whom this book is dedicated—for all their help in so many ways.

Stan Gores
Fond du Lac, Wisconsin

Introduction

I f you can remember the winning smile of Franklin D. Roosevelt or the heartache of watching the funeral procession of John F. Kennedy, you know that presidents touch our lives.

They're not just chief executives, sitting in the White House, far removed from the power of our votes. We put them into office. We replace them. We criticize, or give them praise. We pass judgment on their decisions practically every day. But, most of all, we get to know them.

Depending upon where we live, we may get to see a president in person occasionally, or we may have to settle for watching him on television or reading about him in books, magazines, and newspapers. Few of us, however, are indifferent to the experience of actually seeing a president. We know we are looking at the leader of a country that is regarded as most powerful in the world. And he's just plain "Mr. President"—not His Highness or His Excellency.

We have all seen presidents on inauguration day, looking young and vigorous, filled with hopes. We have seen them later, careworn, the victims of strokes, heart attacks and other serious illnesses. We have even seen them shot down by assassins. And, when many of them leave office, often under heavy pressure from the media, we have seen how the job has turned their hair gray, and how the lines have deepened in their faces. It's not hard to understand why the tasks of the presidency have been called awesome.

Because of our partisan views as free-thinking Americans, sometimes we are happy to see them depart. Or we may be sorry. But whether their record has been good or bad, great or mediocre, they invariably leave the stage of the White House with a certain amount of public admiration. As in the case of President Harry Truman, we generally believe that, successful or not, on our behalf they have "done their damndest."

Over the years, as the office has evolved, our presidents have had some interesting observations of their own about their responsibilities. John Quincy Adams summed up his presidential term: "the most miserable years of my life."

Abraham Lincoln, in his inimitable way, remarked, "I feel like the man who was tarred and feathered and ridden out of town on a rail." To the man who asked him how he liked it, he said, "If it wasn't for the honor of the thing, I'd rather walk."

William Howard Taft said that, as president, he felt he was there "simply to hear other people talk."

But to someone as supercharged as Theodore Roosevelt, the constant challenges of the office were such a delight that he commented, "No other president ever enjoyed the presidency as I did."

No matter how our presidents have looked upon the tasks that the electorate thrust in their direction, it has been difficult for us not to respond to them as human beings.

There was godlike admiration, for example, for George Washington. There was a great sense of common-man charisma surrounding Andrew Jackson. There was hate, mockery, and, in the end, enormous love for Lincoln. There was grief for William McKinley, bully admiration for Teddy Roosevelt, sympathy for the shattered dreams of Woodrow Wilson, sorrow for the shortcomings of Warren Harding, and excessive blame for Herbert Hoover.

The American people, who elected him four times and were lifted with hope by his jaunty, smiling, confident face, believed Franklin D. Roosevelt when he said, "The only thing we have to fear is fear itself." They grew to understand and admire the gutsy bravado of Truman. They liked Dwight "Ike" Eisenhower, and they shed tears to a sad drumbeat when the caisson moved slowly along Washington streets carrying the body of John F. Kennedy. Many felt deceived by Richard Nixon, disappointed by Jimmy Carter; they're still passing judgment on Ronald Reagan.

So our presidents are close to us. In many cases, we feel we know them better than the man or woman who lives just down the street.

And because we all share the presidential experience, we are drawn to the thousands of mementos that were made for our presidents during their campaigns and after they assumed office. That's what this book is all about.

It provides a diversified assortment of presidential and campaign memorabilia—souvenirs and trinkets, treasured pieces, and items of contrasting values. In some way, all have been associated with the presidents and their families.

These mementos have been found everywhere—in antiques shops, in homes, at flea markets, at auctions, and through advertisements. Some have been received as gifts. Others represent costly expenditures. Hundreds are from the collection that my wife, Jeannine, and I have assembled over a period of many years; they're supplemented by items from other collections and by treasures of the Smithsonian Institution. We have always appreciated presidential glass and china. That, it seems, was the propelling interest that kept us hunting for everything else—political buttons, ribbons, medalets, postcards, banks, and so on.

In this much expanded second edition, great emphasis has been placed on political buttons—the rarities as well as those that are still easily found. Buttons, after all, are hunted by more collectors today than any other political items, and for good reason. Graphically, many of them are beautiful, and they also capture in their exciting designs the tumult and the shouting of presidential history. As with most items that are linked with the lives of our chief executives, the value of buttons that are scarce has risen dramatically in recent decades—and the trend continues to be upward.

About Prices

The prices quoted in this book are intended mainly as current guides. Based on extensive study of the field and the counsel of others who have long experience as collectors and sellers, we have tried to come up with figures that are reasonable. In the final analysis, of course, buyers inevitably will rely on their own judgment as to how high they are willing to go to bring something into their collections. As always, the cost of any item still is determined by that old cliché, "It's worth whatever somebody wants to pay." And we all know that the desire to feel close to history can be a mighty force, as any dedicated collector will tell you.

From a personal standpoint, collecting presidential and campaign memorabilia has been a fascinating experience.

I'll never forget the day that I was able to hold in my hands a timeworn Jackson flask, studying the rough pontil, looking at the air bubbles, all the time appreciating that such a glass relic had survived from the era of Andrew Jackson. I felt the same way seeing a variety of presidential items—a Washington clothing button, a Liverpool jug, a rare ferrotype, a beautifully colored jugate campaign button. I know I'll always remember the time when Jeannine spotted Laddie Boy, the handsomely designed metal statue of Warren Harding's famous dog, at an antiques show in Illinois. And memorable, too, are the strikingly imaginative, full-color posters produced for the 1900 campaign of William McKinley and his running mate, Teddy Roosevelt.

Of course, learning about any hobby doesn't come without a certain price. I know of no collectors who haven't occasionally overpaid or who don't regret having bought something in a moment of weakness. The most dramatic example, in my case, in-

A couple of Jackson frogs

volved what used to be reverently known as "the Jackson frog." This heavy iron bullfrog doorstop, bearing the embossed slogan, "I Croak for the Jackson Wagon," for many years enjoyed a prestigious reputation as a rare artifact of the campaigns of Andrew Jackson.

One interpretation was that the wording meant that the frog was croaking as a tribute to voters who were willing to travel by wagon to a Jackson political rally. Pictures of the famous frog doorstop appeared regularly in quality history books and in the listings of the most reputable auction houses in America. Moreover, one of the old frogs even was displayed at the Hermitage, the home of Andrew Jackson in Tennessee, where reproduction likenesses of the frog were sold as souvenirs. So I outbid everyone in a mail auc-

tion and bought my own, paying hundreds of dollars—as had other collectors and museum curators before me. But, alas, in 1980, new research by Herbert Collins of the Smithsonian Institution identified the frogs as having been made not for a spirited political campaign from the distant past, but for a Jackson, Michigan wagon factory in the 1880s. My own checking with a Michigan historian later supported this finding.

That particular learning experience, overriding much weighty evidence that had pointed to the authenticity of the iron frog, came hard not only for me but for many. And, like the others, today I accept the reality of simply owning an unusual advertising item that is more than a century old and still is worth about a hundred dollars as a collectible.

I cite the Jackson frog case merely to illustrate that collecting is a never-ending educational process. Usually the experienced collector will come out ahead. But nobody can own everything. Nobody has the best of everything. And nobody knows everything.

The pursuit of presidential and campaign memorabilia, however, is worth every hour that's devoted to it. If you like history, antiques, collectibles, and the human story of the United States, you'll enjoy collecting mementos of our presidents. And you'll also be joining the ranks of thousands of informed people who share the same enthusiasm.

Welcome to an interesting hobby.

Why Collect Presidential Memorabilia?

THE POLITICAL SITUATION.

An old Thomas Nast cartoon

For every American president, there's a trail of mementos. At times the path may be narrow and almost impossible to find. But the clues of history are there, linked by a huge array of political artifacts that mirror the interesting lives of thirty-nine chief executives—all the way from the worshipful days of George Washington to the bullet-scarred presidency of Ronald Reagan.

Merely looking at a sampling of presidential souvenirs ignites the imagination. An old Boston newspaper reports on the inaugural speech of Thomas Jefferson. A rare ribbon pictures Martin Van Buren. The embossed image of President Franklin Pierce is found on the battered cover of a broken field mirror. The beardless face of Abraham Lincoln looks out beyond time from the ring of an 1860 campaign ferrotype. And a solemn tintype showing Stephen Douglas kindles our thoughts to those grave pre-Civil War days when, as senatorial candidates, Lincoln and Douglas engaged in debates that made history.

Tintype of Stephen A. Douglas

Old advertisements from the pages of *Frank Leslie's Illustrated* newspaper offer "political goods" such as flags, lanterns, and torches, thereby reviving thoughts of dramatic nighttime political campaign parades staged for the controversial election battle between Rutherford B. Hayes and Samuel Tilden. The artistry of Thomas Nast reminds us of the power still wielded by political cartoonists. The stiffly dignified features of Grover Cleveland and James G. Blaine, captured forever on time-crazed ironstone plates, stir memories of their low-road campaign of 1884. The caricatured face of Franklin D. Roosevelt embossed on the side of a pottery pitcher brings back the inspiring personality of the only man ever elected to the presidency four times. And there's a lingering supply of political items to help us remember those brief, poignant Camelot days in the White House before assassin Lee Harvey Oswald, on November 22, 1963, violently ended the life of John F. Kennedy.

Presidential souvenirs also give us an intensely personal record of our national political process. They represent a time when hopes soared or great ambitions slowly dissolved in failure or scandal, a time when slogans were manufactured to glorify or demolish the reputation of a candidate and, sadly, times when as Americans we were cast into periods of deep mourning for a fallen leader.

We're carried on this nostalgic flight into presidential history by a bewildering assortment of mementos—pipes, canes, umbrellas, vases, buttons, watch fobs, statuettes, pitchers, torchlights, medals, tokens, ribbons, postcards, banks, hats, bread trays, jewelry, clocks, posters, stanhopes, ferrotypes, lanterns, bottles, tumblers, serving trays, newspapers, brooches, mugs, badges, and much more. The list seems close to endless. And all of these items have become valued remnants of a few exciting moments that flashed and then faded in our political heritage. They're the tattered shreds of days long gone, fragments of history that often seem as close to us as yesterday, when political parties produced a torrent of colorfully designed souvenirs to capture the minds and hearts of voters.

As we look back, we discover that it's surprising how quickly a president is absorbed by antiquity. After playing such an important role in our lives, suddenly he's gone. And that's why all these collectibles easily fall under the heading Presidential Memorabilia.

Choosing which direction to go is a decision that is made by the individual collector. While there has long been keen interest in cleverly conceived buttons turned out for our election campaigns, there are still great opportunities for collectors to also acquire other exciting relics from presidential elections. Many, in fact, provide fertile territory for collectors.

For example, even though their roots are deep in our election history, medalets and tokens have remained good buys for alert hobbyists. Medalets from the campaign of William H. Harrison in 1840, especially, still are reasonably priced, primarily because many have remained available. Campaign ribbons from the 1880s and thereafter also appear on the market frequently. The same can be said for some colorful bandannas. Excellent paper souvenirs of the presidents are often sold at bargain prices. And outstanding glass and ceramic collectibles that feature our presidential candidates—their images, slogans, and party symbols—still can be found. Worth mentioning are the colored elephant and donkey figural bottles made for the 1968 campaign that matched Richard Nixon against Hubert Humphrey. These and other comparatively new presidential bottles, made by the Wheaton Glass Company of Millville, New Jersey, are well worth the modest prices usually found on them in shops and at flea markets. In fact, some of the highest-quality historical glass produced in this country was inspired by presidential campaigns. The Classic

Pattern plates designed for the 1884 election by a long-admired but obscure Philadelphia moldmaker, P. J. Jacobus, are outstanding examples.

While inexpensive sleepers still can be found in nearly all presidential categories, there are certain artifacts dating back to our early presidents—and some rarities from campaigns that came much later—that deservedly elicit extravagant prices. Liverpool pitchers bearing the likenesses of Washington, John Adams, Thomas Jefferson, and James Madison usually bring anywhere from around $1,500 to $2,500, even when not in the best condition. A sulphide brooch of Martin Van buren sold as far back as 1981 for $2,500. The sale of scarce ferrotypes and buttons for hundreds of dollars is not uncommon. And at an auction in New York in 1981, a 1920 black-and-white jugate button picturing James Cox for president and Franklin Roosevelt for vice president set a dazzling record when it brought $30,000 plus a buyer's fee of $3,000. The preauction estimate on that button, which had sold for $5,800 in 1976 and has been hailed as the only one of its kind, was $10,000. The value of other Cox buttons, not as rare as the record-breaker, certainly has not been damaged since that 1981 sale. But the point to remember is that rarity, condition, the affluence of buyers, and even the emotional levels of an auction audience are all factors that help determine prices. The smart collector adjusts according to personal circumstances.

So, for anyone who enjoys American history or, more specifically, politics, collecting presidential memorabilia is an enormously interesting and educational hobby. It offers the opportunity to specialize in certain elections, favorite candidates, parties, and preferred collectibles. The choice is determined by whatever a collector may find appealing and, to an extent, the amount of money available for spending.

Beginning collectors often can start right at home, searching through drawers, boxes, attics, basements, and storerooms. Discoveries sometimes can be astounding, especially if a family has shown prior political interest. From there, the hobbyist advances to flea markets, household sales, rummage sales and antiques shops. In addition, there are well stocked auction catalogs offered by knowledgeable dealers plus antiques and hobby publications filled with advertising. There is also the American Political Items Collectors (APIC) organization, which provides members with well-researched information and the opportunity to attend state, regional, and national meetings where much buying, selling, and trading is assured. And, finally, many collectors have enjoyed getting involved in the national political convention process—where some excellent collectibles originate.

There are collectors, of course, who recognize that presidential Americana has been rising steadily in value and who therefore consider entering the picture strictly as an investment. After all, investing in

antiques is nothing new. People have been collecting everything from folk art to beer cans with a goal of ultimately turning a profit.

Most collectors I know, however, do not rank investment as their top motivating priority. While fully aware of rising prices and delighted to see their political mementos grow in financial stature, they are more enthralled over the ownership of items that they can appreciate from a historic sense. They enjoy having something in their possession that dates back to an interesting presidential era. Even an old souvenir china pin-tray showing a picture of the President's Mansion can set them wondering who might have occupied the White House when the tray was made.

While acquiring presidential items and watching them increase in value, collectors also enjoy a fascinating learning experience. A modest achievement, perhaps—but how many friends do you know who can rattle off all the names of United States presidents in order, usually without stumbling? And how many know the names of the six presidents who held the office in the hectic 12-year span from 1841 to 1853? Hundreds of collectors recite the list without trouble.

The most effective presidential Americana collectors, in fact, are those who study the history of our elections and become familiar with the names of the candidates—losers as well as winners—and who train themselves to recognize, not only by name but by face, as many of the participants in our presidential parade as possible. Good button collectors, particularly, can profit from this kind of recognition factor and save many dollars in building an impressive collection.

But it's not button collectors alone who benefit from studied familiarity with the presidential cast of characters. An example is the woman who, while making the rounds at a summer flea market, spotted a little clear glass plate with a lacy border. In the center of the plate was the unidentified portrait of a man. The price was low, and the woman bought it.

"I've never been able to figure out whose picture that is on the plate," said the dealer.

"It's William McKinley," the lady replied, proudly holding her underpriced acquisition. It was a campaign plate, and she knew it. At home she had a similar plate showing the face of William Jennings Bryan.

So, as in all fields, knowing how to zero in on the good buys provides the collector with a significant money-saving advantage.

This also leads us to those who occasionally are frightened away by vague observations that prices are too high and "political items are hard to find." The material is still out there, in tantalizing variety, waiting to be discovered—frequently at bargain-basement prices. Moreover, collecting presidential memorabilia allows a smooth blending of the old and the comparatively inexpensive new as presidents come and go in the White House.

Thousands who already collect presidential mementos have found it to be a rewarding, satisfying, and intellectually stimulating hobby. But most of all, it's just plain fun.

Getting Started with Buttons

Although the variation of things yet to be found may be staggering, it's usually an eye-catching political button that gets a collector started. Thousands of buttons just seem to keep popping up from everywhere.

Some are valued in the hundreds of dollars. Others occasionally stimulate buyers to pay into the thousands. Yet most of the buttons that are out there have remained inexpensive, often going for only a few dollars. And amazing discoveries are still being made.

One veteran collector proved it in Milwaukee a couple of years ago when he spotted a rare James Cox button from the 1920 presidential election. The dealer was happy to sell it for $4. Its true value to collectors is close to $500.

Obviously, miracles still happen. But the neophyte collector who ventures into the hobby in pursuit of good buttons and other desirable items should be armed with the best weapon a collector can have—knowledge. After all, button competition can be tough and, at times, seemingly relentless. And the most successful button collectors have one thing in common—they're aggressive.

So beginners who trust to luck, or who downgrade the importance of really learning about buttons, run the costly risk of missing many of the bargains. What's more, they face the pitfall of wasting money on buttons that are overpriced or are only reproductions.

A factor that works in favor of the collector is that the supply of buttons is somewhat bewildering to the sellers in antiques shops and at flea markets. Dealers have such a variety of items to handle that it's difficult for them to determine the true value of every button. So they sometimes undercharge, as in the case of the Cox button previously mentioned. When that happens, a collector has to possess the expertise to know that opportunity is knocking. Conversely, a collector has to know when opportunity isn't knocking, too.

Dinner pail button, 1900

Cox button, 1920

For example, a dealer may assume that a common button from one of President McKinley's campaigns must be valuable because it's old. Not so. Many are no more valuable than some of the better buttons from recent campaigns. The collector must be careful not to confuse antiquity with rarity. Knowing something about the history of political buttons and their value is the place to start.

9

It might be said that buttons have roots all the way back to George Washington. At the time of his inauguration in 1789, clothing buttons were produced bearing the slogan, "Long Live the President." These were not "campaign" buttons. Actually, there was no campaign at that time. The buttons were simply clothing buttons made to honor Washington.

Another type of clothing button surfaced some years later. These were known as "backname buttons," with the name of the president inscribed on the back of a standard gilt-front button. Presidents whose names have become associated with backname buttons include James Monroe, Andrew Jackson, Martin Van Buren, and William H. Harrison, with a half-dozen or more variations found for Jackson. Such buttons also were manufactured for a presidential campaign loser, Henry Clay. Embossed brass clothing buttons later trailed the backnames for such candidates as Harrison, Zachary Taylor, James Garfield, and others.

Among additional predecessors of today's campaign buttons were the attractive medalets made for presidential candidates as far back as the 1820s. Medalets, as well as tokens with political themes, often are found with holes which allowed voters to attach them to their clothing as a sign of support.

With the growth of photography, it was only natural that tintypes would become an important part of the early campaign process. Many Americans have tintypes of deceased relatives, and even these have become collectibles. But when you find them with images of some of our Civil War–period presidential candidates, such as Abraham Lincoln, they acquire new and significant historical value. Political collectors call them *ferrotypes,* and those pieces that have survived in good condition are keenly sought after and treasured.

At the time of the 1888 election between Grover Cleveland and Benjamin Harrison, there was successful experimentation with celluloid, but well-made celluloid buttons—the kind that collectors so eagerly seek today—did not start to appear in quantity until 1896. That's when William McKinley and William Jennings Bryan hooked up in the exciting campaign that is remembered for a controversial issue, gold versus silver.

Designed with imagination, wit and the full flavor of turn-of-the-century politics, the attractive and often beautiful buttons caught the public fancy almost immediately. Moreover, as pinbacks, they were easy to wear. You simply pinned them on your clothing, and wherever you went you proudly let the whole world see the name of your political favorite. Who knows what heated political discussions may have been generated by the wearing of a button!

Many of the early buttons were manufactured by the Whitehead & Hoag Company of Newark, New Jersey; but others of high quality also were turned out by Bastian Bros. of Rochester, New York and the St.

Jugate celluloid, 1904

Louis Button Company of St. Louis, Missouri. Voters were interested in their government, and the buttons found a ready market. Buoyed by good sales, the button designers outdid themselves with catchy themes and considerable artistic ingenuity.

It can be said that button production flourished from 1896 to about 1912. People liked them. Moreover, being rich in graphics, with the finest of colors, such buttons were worth saving—and many Americans saved them. They were tossed into drawers or boxes, their owners vaguely aware that the buttons would preserve a moment in presidential history. Those that escaped moisture and other damage today are showcased in some of the best collections in the country.

Around 1920, the old celluloid buttons began to be replaced by buttons that were lithographed, with the color and design printed directly on tin instead of the paper that had been protected by celluloid. It's true that celluloid-type buttons still are made, but actually acetate rather than celluloid is being used.

As anyone who follows politics knows, the use of buttons for campaign purposes is far from over. But the amount of funding available for buttons and other campaign trinkets has been reduced. These days, candidates like to plow millions into well-packaged television where they can get pumped-up exposure before millions of viewers.

Nevertheless, plenty of buttons are still in circulation, although they're frequently made in larger sizes and with more simplicity than the old-time pinbacks. In a few cases, today's designers have had the good judgment to look back at those old beauties from the past and have tried to duplicate them. That kind of flattery, in itself, says something about the quality that has helped make McKinley and Bryan famous among today's collectors.

So what do you look for in a good button?

You look for good design. Lively color. You look for rarities—buttons you don't often see. You look for "jugates"—buttons that show both the presidential and vice presidential candidates. You look for "picture" buttons that feature the candidates because you know they are more desirable than those limited to

The Language of Button Collectors

Ambrotype. An early type photograph, with a glass negative backed by a dark surface so as to appear positive. Rare in the political field.

APIC. These are initials that stand for an organization called the American Political Items Collectors, devoted to research and information that is helpful to collectors. For membership information, write to: APIC, Secretary-Treasurer Joseph Hayes, P.O. Box 340339, San Antonio, Texas 78234.

Brummagem. The word means "showy or cheap" and is used by some political collectors to indicate items of low value, such as a button that is merely a copy of an original.

Celluloid Button. Made its appearance in abundance during the 1896 presidential campaign. Celluloid was used to cover the button design, which was printed on paper. Slang term: *cello.*

Collar. Celluloid buttons have a supportive metal rim on the back. (This is a potential damage point on some of the old buttons because of rust.) The collar also is referred to as the *collet* or *flange.*

Ferrotypes. These are tintypes that grew in popularity as campaign items in the era of Abraham Lincoln and for a number of years thereafter. Delicate, but excellent mementos.

Foxing. This is the word used by collectors to describe the dark moisture marks frequently found on old celluloid buttons. Foxing lessens the value of a button.

Graphics. This term includes the designs, slogans and colors used to create an image on political buttons and other items as well.

Jugate. Buttons that feature the pictures of both the presidential and vice presidential candidates. These are especially desired by collectors.

Lithograph Buttons. The lithograph process for buttons took hold around 1920, with designs and slogans printed directly on tin. Lithograph buttons do not require collars. Just as foxing damages celluloid buttons, scratches mar lithographs.

Mechanicals. These are political pins that were made to feature a special movement, such as the wings of an eagle pin opening to reveal the pictures of the candidates. There were a number of different versions, attractively framed in shell badges.

Medalets. This generally applies to numismatic pieces that picture a presidential candidate and often his running mate, and they are well under two inches in diameter. When they get beyond that size, they merit a different numismatic classification. Many collectors have a tendency to erroneously lump medalets with "tokens."

Paper Photo. With the development of photography, cardboard photos began to replace tintypes in early campaign items, such as shell badges.

Pinbacks. The name given to buttons that have a common pin used to fasten them to a lapel or sweater. Pinbacks became popular in the 1896 election and have remained popular to this day.

Repros. Short for the word *reproduction.* Repros are the items such as political buttons that are manufactured to look like the originals. Button collectors should learn to identify repros—and always check the small print on the rim and on the back when buying a button.

Shell Badges. Tintypes and cardboard photos of presidential candidates were framed in shell badges—which were often artfully stamped from sheets of brass. Shell badges came in many designs, both patriotic and political, and added much interest to the mechanicals.

Slogan Buttons. Thousands of political buttons were manufactured to carry slogans, especially during the era of Franklin Roosevelt. An example is the button that said of FDR's wife, "We Don't Want Eleanor Either." Collectors usually rank these below picture buttons in value.

Studs. Made to wear on the lapel of a political advocate, studs fit neatly into buttonholes and were produced in a wide variety. They had great popularity in the 1890s. Although attractive, they have not been collected with the same zest as buttons.

Sulphide Brooches. Dating back to the era of Andrew Jackson, Martin Van Buren and William H. Harrison, sulphide brooches are impressive additions to any collection. The cameo images contrast richly with colored surfaces under glass and are highlighted by ornate little frames. In good condition, these are costly not only because of the presidential antiquity but because of the quality as well.

Tokens. Often confused with political medalets, tokens generally stress themes, such as the "hard times" tokens that flayed Andrew Jackson and served as issue-oriented keepsakes. Tokens also have been symbols, and in the Civil War era many served as a substitute for money. However, because some have been tied closely to politics, they have value as presidential collectibles.

Musical button, 1985

slogans. You look for buttons in various sizes, because some sizes are scarce. You look for buttons in the best condition that you can find them. And you look for buttons that picture the also-rans, the candidates who gave the presidential race their best shot but didn't make it. Sometimes you'll be amazed at the value of buttons picturing losers—such as Eugene Debs, Charles Evans Hughes, James M. Cox and others.

You have to recognize, too, that buttons that are damaged don't have the same marketability as buttons that are a little closer to perfect. Scars from moisture or rust, cracks, scratches, or lumps all cause a button to be downgraded. When the damage is slight,

there are times when it's wise to ignore it. But collectors have to be wary and use good judgment.

As in every other worthwhile endeavor, you don't learn good judgment in a day. You cultivate it wisely through study, familiarity with the market, going to antiques shows, flea markets, and auctions. You expand your collecting experience in every way that you can, and you join helpful organizations such as the American Political Items Collectors. Eventually, good judgment in collecting becomes the rule rather than the exception.

It should be said, too, that, while some collectors specialize in buttons, there are many other presidential items to be found along the way, as the wide diversity of photos in this book clearly shows. Don't overlook them. Not only do they help round out a collection, but they become a highly interesting and valuable collection in themselves.

So buttons—old and new—represent a great starting point for the collector, whether they go back to that solemn battle between McKinley and Bryan or only as far as the high-tech age of the musical button picturing Ronald Reagan and George Bush. From a few decades ago, when they were still struggling to earn respect as legitimate collectibles, political buttons have come a long way.

Scarcity Years for Collectors, 1789–1828

cquiring a rare item that dates back to the presidency of George Washington is an extremely difficult and often costly mission. However, collectors are fortunate in that thousands of excellent commemorative items have been manufactured in his honor.

Rarity is not confined only to Washington, however. Just about everything from our first six presidents is in that category. It's true that items from Washington, John Adams, Thomas Jefferson, James Madison, James Monroe, and John Quincy Adams come onto the market occasionally. But since everyone treasures relics from these early leaders, they generally are regarded as first-rate museum-quality and are expensive.

Metal clothing buttons are associated with Washington's inauguration, which took place on April 30, 1789 on the balcony of Federal Hall in New York City. After administering the oath of office to Washington, the chancellor of the state of New York said, "Long live George Washington, the president of the United States." Perhaps as a reference to the chancellor's remark, buttons were made with the inscription, "Long Live the President." There have been reproductions since then, but original buttons in good condition sell for hundreds of dollars today.

After Washington's death at the age of 67 on December 14, 1799, British potters recognized the sales potential among mourning Americans. They began using Washington's image as a profitable decoration on the wares that they exported to this country. As a result, our first president is pictured on Liverpool pitchers, mugs, plates, and platters, Battersea curtain tiebacks, and other items. All the early nineteenth-

Washington Apotheosis pitcher dating from about 1802.

century items are rare, or at least scarce, and create somewhat of a clamor when offered for sale.

Nevertheless, because he has always remained "first in the hearts of his countrymen," Washington souvenirs have been perpetuated in huge quantities, and hundreds well qualify for any presidential collection. One side of many early flasks, for example, shows the embossed likeness of Washington, even when the flasks were made to exalt other distinguished Americans such as Andrew Jackson and Zachary Taylor.

During the time of our great 1876 Centennial, too, there was an impressive Washington boom. The face of our first president appeared on mugs, pitchers, vases, match holders, medals, bread trays, and a wide assortment of other Centennial souvenirs. While these items may not be comparable to the clothing buttons that were worn at the time Washington was still alive, they are already more than a century old and thereby can be classified as antiques. Collectors of presidential memorabilia are wise to look for them and to recognize their status when they are found.

When Washington refused a third term and set a precedent that was to endure until Franklin D. Roosevelt broke it in 1940, he created the first presidential vacancy. It was filled with the election of his vice president, John Adams, who took office on March 4, 1797. Unfortunately, with the exception of an extreme rarity or two, there is almost nothing to be found by collectors from the Adams presidency even though he and his wife, Abigail, were the first occupants of the president's house. Incidentally, Adams set a proper atmosphere when he wrote, "May none but honest and wise men ever rule under this roof." Yet despite a dearth of souvenirs, there are ways to fill the gap for the term of Adams, since collectors are able to rely on early lithographs and such items as the aged silhouette pictured in this book.

The talented Jefferson, whom history tells us was not an impressive speaker, was a profound thinker and writer, to say nothing of his inventions. Today, those who can afford it try to acquire documents bearing his signature. But there are also Liverpool pitchers and mugs available, and there's even a rare inauguration medal. Moreover, because Jefferson executed the Louisiana Purchase, numerous items that commemorate that event show his likeness. For the collector, such commemoratives often are not that expensive, yet many are attractive and provide a good representation of the Jefferson presidency, which lasted from March 4, 1801 to March 3, 1809.

President Madison, who served from March 4, 1809 to March 3, 1817, was in office at the time the British burned the White House. His courageous wife, Dolley, saved many valuable articles from destruction, including the famous portrait of George Washington. That episode, in addition to her great charm, is why it often seems that we hear more about Dolley Madison than the president himself. Yet for collectors who can afford them, there are pitchers that portray Madison. Just about anything that collectors can find that pictures Madison makes a worthy addition to a presidential collection.

Rarity is also the word for the presidency of James Monroe, March 4, 1817, to March 3, 1825. He is best remembered, of course, for the Monroe Doctrine which was set forth in 1823. There are two mugs that appear on rare occasions, with one spelling Monroe's name correctly and the other listing it as "Munroe." Either makes a prestigious display for a collector.

John Quincy Adams, the only president whose father also held the office, was a winner in the much disputed election of 1824. Although Andrew Jackson led the four-man field with a popular vote of 151,271 to 113,122, no candidate received a majority of the electoral votes, and the election went into the House of Representatives. There, the supporters of third-place finisher Henry Clay rallied behind Adams, giving him the election. This did all the more to spur on the followers of Jackson, who dedicated themselves to getting him into the White House in 1828. The emotion surrounding this race perhaps contributed to the increase in campaign souvenirs turned out for the Jackson campaign.

Memorabilia from the presidency of John Quincy Adams, March 4, 1825 to March 3, 1829, has remained extremely hard to find. There are some medals, a fabric, a round pewter-rimmed engraving under glass, thread boxes that carry slogans on the cover with a picture of Adams on the inside, and an extremely rare flask that shows his embossed image. Obviously, all these items are costly. However, because John Quincy Adams had a remarkable public service career, he has not been ignored by the souvenir makers. His likeness can be found on paper goods and in a fine Currier print.

By the time Jackson was elected in 1828, the idea of producing more and more political items to promote candidates was on the way to becoming tradition. The American voter was now becoming deeply involved, and many were willing to campaign in an effort to get their man into the White House. Nobody really knew it then, but the colorful political process as we know it today, characterized by parades, speeches, hoopla, and campaign souvenirs, had begun to emerge.

Jackson to Hayes, 1829–1880

Although the candidacy of Andrew Jackson had a catalytic impact on the production of mementos for presidential campaigns, souvenirs from "Old Hickory" have remained somewhat elusive for thousands of today's political collectors.

Jackson, whose two terms kept him in the White House from March 4, 1829, to March 3, 1837, is remembered today by snuffboxes, bandannas, fabric patterns, engravings under glass, thread boxes, clothing buttons, tokens, ribbons, flasks, plates, and some handsome luster pitchers.

All of these items shout the drama of our early presidential campaign history and, for those who make the pursuit, still can be found. Occasionally, they're discovered in antiques shops and, if you're lucky, at large flea markets. But the best sources probably are political mail auctions, where first-rate items continue to go to the highest bidders. Buyers have to be prepared, financially and otherwise, on such occasions because the enthusiasm for collecting presidential memorabilia increases every year.

An erratic pattern that typifies political souvenir production is shown by the shortage of collectibles from the presidency of Martin Van Buren, Jackson's successor. Little Van, our eighth president, defeated not only William Henry Harrison in the election of 1836, but also such a formidable opponent as Daniel Webster, who ran under the Whig party banner.

Among the items from Van Buren, who was inaugurated March 4, 1837 and served until March 3, 1841, are ribbons, snuffboxes, tokens, Currier prints, medalets, anti-Van Buren mechanical cards, and some beautiful sulphide brooches. As in the case of most of our early presidents, the collector has to be prepared to pay well for most items that were made in Van Buren's lifetime.

Many mark the election of William Henry Harrison in 1840 as the real beginning of presidential campaigns. His supporters pulled out all stops in

Old lithograph of John Tyler

providing paraphernalia to get him elected. It's ironic that he became ill and died after being in the White House for only a month. Until the inauguration of Ronald Reagan 140 years later, Harrison, at age 68, had been the oldest man ever inaugurated when he took office on March 4, 1841.

His slogan had been "Tippecanoe and Tyler too," which not only served to remind Americans that he had defeated Chief Tecumseh at Tippecanoe Creek, but also boosted the image of his running mate, John Tyler.

Despite his brief moment on the presidential scene, Harrison today is remembered by hundreds of souvenirs, including everything from a variety of log cabin clothing, buttons to tokens, silhouettes, cup plates, snuffboxes, hair brushes, ribbons, sulphide brooches, medalets, reverse painting on glass, spoons, bandannas, song books, banners, pitchers, luster pieces, and the well-known Columbian Star dinnerware. Many of these excellent mementos are still reasonably priced and give collectors the opportunity to reach far into the past to enliven their displays with real historic perspective.

With Tyler elevated to the White House by the death of Harrison, it's not surprising that there is an extremely limited supply of souvenirs from his term in office. He became president on April 6, 1841, the first vice president to fill such a vacancy. Detractors sometimes referred to him as "His Accidency." Tyler's 51-year-old wife, Letitia, died while he was in office, and in June of 1844 he remarried, thereby setting another presidential precedent. His second wife was 24-year-old Julia Gardiner.

There's a rare Tyler ribbon and some prints that can be found, but there's not much else for anyone searching for souvenirs from his years in the White House. However, because he was on the Whig ticket with Harrison, he also shares the spotlight on a number of items that were made when he ran as vice president in 1840.

James K. Polk, who had served as Speaker of the House and was regarded as an expansionist, assumed the presidency on March 4, 1845 and served until March 3, 1849, choosing not to seek reelection. There are interesting ribbons that recall the candidacy of Polk and George Dallas, who ran as Polk's vice president. Among other artifacts are a song book, a picture under glass framed in pewter, tokens, medalets, and colored lithographs. Scarcity also keeps Polk items generally high in price.

When the nation turned to Mexican War–hero General Zachary Taylor, known as "Old Rough and Ready," the output of campaign items again quickened. Taylor, who served from March 4, 1849 until his death on July 9, 1850, became the second chief executive to die in the White House. He is remembered by a series of flasks, lithographs under glass, campaign newspapers, posters, cartoons, snuffboxes, reverse painting on glass, bandannas, razors, fabric patterns, medalets, clothing buttons, a clay pipe, mirrors, and ribbons. However, despite the variety of these items, they remain hard to find.

Taylor's death propelled his vice president, Millard Fillmore, into the White House. Fillmore served from July 10, 1850 until March 3, 1853, having suffered a defeat in his effort to win the nomination of his party.

John Fremont medalet, 1856

Finding Fillmore collectibles also is quite difficult, although there is a paperweight made by the New England Glass Company, in addition to a pewter-rimmed picture under glass, Currier prints, textiles, a parade lantern, medalets, ballots, and ribbons. Most of these items were produced for his later unsuccessful bid for the presidency in 1856.

Succeeding Fillmore in the election of 1852 was a democratic darkhorse, Franklin Pierce, who defeated the Whig candidate, General Winfield Scott. His term of office was from March 4, 1853 to March 3, 1857. Souvenirs of the Pierce administration are scarce indeed, with a field mirror, a few medalets, a ribbon or two, and paper collectibles about all that seem to surface, and then rarely.

In 1856, in the wake of the Kansas-Nebraska Act, the newly founded Republican Party nominated John C. Fremont, who was defeated by James Buchanan, a bachelor nominated by the democrats. During Buchanan's term, from March 4, 1857 to March 3, 1861, tensions continued to mount that ultimately were to lead to the Civil War.

Collectibles from the Buchanan years include ribbons, political tickets, broadsides, flags, and numismatic items. All make desirable additions to any assortment of presidential Americana, as do the ribbons and other campaign items turned out to boost the candidacy of Fremont.

Slavery and sectionalism had become the issues by the time of the 1860 campaign, with the South threatening secession if the nation elected a republican. The northern democrats nominated Stephen A. Douglas; the republicans favored Abraham Lincoln. Other candidates during that stormy year were John C. Breckenridge, who carried the banner of the southern democrats, and John Bell, the candidate for the Constitutional Union.

Lincoln, of course, won the election, taking office on March 4, 1861. He was reelected in 1864. The great Emancipator guided the nation through the bloody years of the Civil War and preserved the Union. Yet for some, that was not enough. He was assassinated by John Wilkes Booth on April 14, 1865. Although we

Postcard showing Lincoln's home on the day of his funeral

often remember him as "Old Abe," Lincoln was only 56 years old at the time that he was gunned down—the first of our presidents slain in office.

Almost anything from the Lincoln presidency is held in high esteem by collectors everywhere, and many specialize in Lincoln items. Fortunately, there is much memorabilia from the days of this great president in addition to some excellent commemorative material. There are flags, broadsides, lanterns, song books, lithographs, Parian ware, plates, cups, torchlights, bandannas, ribbons, banners, tickets, ambrotypes, ferrotypes, medalets, posters, shell badges, vases, and numerous other items. Outstanding glass Lincoln statuettes, in milk-white and frosted crystal, also were produced by the Gillinder & Sons firm of Philadelphia at the time of the 1876 Centennial. These also merit a high place in any collection.

With the death of Lincoln, the vice president, Andrew Johnson, a one-time tailor, assumed the burdens of the postwar presidency. His new power soon touched off quarrels between the president and the republican leadership over the sensitive issue of Reconstruction. Johnson's political enemies started impeachment proceedings against him, but on May 26, 1868, he was acquitted. His term in office was from April 15, 1865 to March 3, 1869.

Unfortunately, little in the way of souvenirs exists from the presidency of Andrew Johnson other than those associated with his campaign as vice president with Lincoln. Collectors hunt for lithographs and whatever other material they can find to help fill the gap.

Civil War hero General Ulysses S. Grant was elected in 1868 and served two undistinguished terms, from March 4, 1869 to March 3, 1877. Enormously popular when he took office, Grant was not as effective in the White House as he'd been on the battlefield. Newspapers were filled with stories of political corruption.

In his campaign for reelection in 1872, Grant also faced the challenge of Victoria C. Woodhull. The first

WHERE THE SHOE PINCHES.

PRESIDENT GRANT—" *Now, Fish, you tell those fellows in Congress that the place was presented to me as a sinecure, and when I've left it, or where I've gone, or what I've done away from Washington, is none of their business! The next thing, I suppose, they'll be inquiring into my cigar bills!*"

woman ever to be so honored, she had been nominated at the National Woman Suffrage Association convention in New York. Her running mate on the People's Party ticket was Frederick Douglass, the first black ever nominated for the vice presidency.

Mementos of Grant's presidency are many and cover just about everything. There are canes, medals, ferrotypes, lithographs, textiles, ribbons, match holders, lanterns, bread trays, plates, Parian ware, badges, jasperware, flags, clothing buttons, posters, and political tickets. Some of the medalets still are reasonably priced, as are "The Patriot and Soldier" and other glass plates.

Adding fuel to the stories of administrative corruption during the mid-1870s, while the nation was preparing to celebrate its first 100 years of freedom, were charges of dirty work in the election of 1876 between republican Rutherford B. Hayes and democrat Samuel J. Tilden. For months, the outcome of the voting remained in doubt, with the electoral commission later deciding strictly along party lines to give the disputed vote to Hayes. This was done despite the fact that Tilden had won the popular vote with a plurality in excess of 250,000. Consequently, even though he was not a party to whatever shenanigans might have gone on, the new president was nicknamed "Rutherfraud."

Finding souvenirs reminiscent of the 1876 campaign, which placed Hayes in office from March 4, 1877 to March 3, 1881, is not easy, but many items do exist. They include canes, lithographs, flags, mugs, ribbons, ferrotypes, badges, pins, plaques, lanterns, ballots, bandannas, songsters, a miniature toby, and other assorted items. Some of the Hayes souvenirs link his candidacy to the 1876 Centennial and thereby have a double significance for collectors.

President and Mrs. Hayes were the parents of eight children and restored the White House to the good graces of the people, even though there were critics who resented the strait-laced manner in which "Lemonade Lucy" ran the executive mansion. The president and his wife observed their silver wedding anniversary while in the White House and, despite the controversial start to his administration, for the most part Hayes earned the respect of Congress and the nation. He decided, however, that one term had been enough. He did not seek reelection in 1880.

The Years of Plenty, 1880–1912

H aving observed the skills and productive capacity of many other countries during the Centennial Exhibition in 1876, factories in the United States had stepped up their own manufacturing tempo by 1880, the year that republican James A. Garfield was elected president. The productive vigor that they displayed contributed to the abundance of souvenirs that marked our colorful presidential process.

Tragedy awaited Garfield, however, and his days as chief executive were short, lasting only from March 4, 1881 until September 19, 1881. He was the victim of assassin Charles Julius Guiteau who shot the president July 2, 1881 at a Washington railway depot. Yet despite the brief time that he was in office, there are many mementos from Garfield's presidency. Some were made for his campaign, and many were made as commemoratives.

These include little glass mugs with his embossed image, one with Chester A. Arthur's name on the handle and another with the date of Garfield's death. Found in addition are a martyr's mug on which he is pictured with Lincoln, plates, badges, ferrotypes, ribbons, textiles, collar boxes, an ABC plate, a song book, medalets, Garfield Drape pattern glass, a mechanical nose-thumbing pin, clothing buttons, and a large amount of paper material. Garfield also is shown on a rare pink luster vase, a delicate but brightly colored Wedgwood pitcher, a majolica pitcher, and a Bennington-type pitcher, among others.

A courageous, well-educated man, Garfield was the fourth president to die in office and the second to become the victim of an assassin. What contributions he might have made will never be known. But on September 20, 1881 his vice president, Chester A. Arthur, moved into the presidency and served until March 3, 1885. However, Arthur was not nominated by the republicans in 1884, and there are few souvenirs from

Wedgwood pitcher honors Garfield

his days in the political spotlight. Among items most commonly found are an ironstone plate with his transfer image, produced for the Garfield campaign, and a collar box that also was made for the 1880 election year.

Grover Cleveland, who once had been a sheriff, was the democratic candidate in 1884, running against the republican "Plumed Knight," James G. Blaine. General Edward S. Bragg, who nominated Cleveland in a fiery and memorable speech, said, "They love him most for the enemies he has made." But it was a low-level campaign, perhaps the dirtiest in history. Cleveland, a bachelor, was accused of being an occasionally hard drinker, and the nation was shocked by the undenied charge that he had fathered an illegitimate child. Blaine's own marital background was sullied, however, and his political ethics were found to be lacking. He was tagged as being anti-Catholic, even though his own sister was the mother superior at a convent in Indiana. This tag was given when he did not instantly back away from a remark made by one of his supporters that the democrats were a party of "rum, Romanism, and rebellion." When this no-holds-barred campaign finally ended, Cleveland had been elected to his first of two nonconsecutive terms. He served from March 4, 1885 to March 3, 1889, during which time, at age 49, he married Frances Folsom, the 22-year-old daughter of his former law partner.

In 1888, although he had performed ably during his first term and had a plurality of more than 90,000 votes, Cleveland lost the election to Benjamin Harrison by virtue of the concept that the electoral college, rather than the people, selects the president.

Collectibles from Cleveland, who defeated Harrison in a rematch in 1892 and served again from March 4, 1893 until March 3, 1897, are not difficult to find. His second term came during the time of the great Columbian Exposition in Chicago, so some things are related to that event. Among souvenirs of Cleveland's two terms in the White House are pipes, bandannas, stanhopes, razors, pillboxes, campaign hats, lanterns, canes, bottles, cigars, match holders, belt buckles, paperweights, plates, pitchers, ribbons, tiles, badges, buttons, and other assorted items. The Classic Pattern glass plates made for his 1884 campaign rank as perhaps the most artistically perfect ever produced.

Harrison, the grandson of William H. Harrison, capitalized on that relationship and revived the old log cabin theme identified with his grandfather. He served from March 4, 1889 to March 3, 1893, when such controversial issues as tariff legislation, the demands of veterans, free coinage, and agrarian unrest dimmed his chances for a second term. Harrison also suffered the loss of his wife, Caroline, who died in 1892. At age 62, he remarried in 1896, taking as his second wife 37-year-old widow Mary Dimmick.

Included among the great variety of souvenirs from the presidency of Harrison are well-designed jugate glass bread trays, song books, ribbons, canes, watches, whistles, stanhopes, match holders, umbrellas, a puzzle, cartoons, posters, fabrics, badges, top hats, plates, mechanical pins, tiles, paperweights, statuettes, a bisque novelty item, and many other collectibles.

By the time William McKinley squared off against William Jennings Bryan in 1896, the campaign process was in full sway, including the tactic of using trains for whistle-stops. The first celluloid buttons began to appear, and Americans everywhere seemed to want to wear them to show their political choice. The key issue in this battle was free coinage of silver and the gold standard, with Bryan's "Cross of Gold" speech one of the most famous ever delivered at a convention. But McKinley, campaigning mostly from

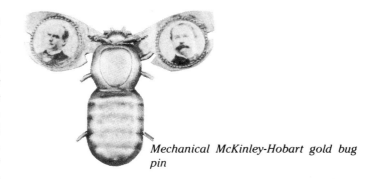

Mechanical McKinley-Hobart gold bug pin

his front porch in Ohio, won the election. He took office for his first term on March 4, 1897 and defeated Bryan a second time in 1900 by a larger plurality after the American success in the Spanish-American War. McKinley became the third president to be assassinated when he was shot by an anarchist, Leon Czolgosz, while attending the Pan-American Exposition in Buffalo, New York on September 6, 1901. He died a week later.

The number of items made for McKinley is immense. Some say that because so many of us have merely stumbled across McKinley souvenirs that he is perhaps more responsible than anyone else for the growing horde of political collectors that exists today. McKinley is found not only on a fine assortment of beautifully colored celluloid buttons, but also on bread trays, pitchers, cups and saucers, ribbons, badges, tumblers, canes, clocks, serving trays, mechanical gold bugs, shot glasses, and bandannas—just to give a reasonable sampling. The same may be said, of course, for the tons of campaign items made for Bryan, who turned out to be a three-time loser.

With McKinley's death, his vice president, the ebullient Theodore Roosevelt, acceded to the White House. Sworn in on September 14, 1901, he was elected to a full term in 1904 and served until March 3, 1909. Roosevelt helped establish the United States as a world power, and he still ranks as one of the most charismatic presidents in our history. An attempt was made on his life in Milwaukee on October 14, 1912. Even though he was hit by the bullet of would-be assassin John Schrank, he still made a speech that same night and went on to a full recovery. Like Cleveland, he came back for another try at the presidency after being out of office, but unlike Cleveland, he failed.

Because of his long involvement in politics, there are many souvenirs that mark Roosevelt's career. Included are buttons, watch fobs, bandannas, serving trays, banks, spoons, plates, banners, flags, pipes, purses, pocket knives, scissors, razors, paperweights, ribbons, pins, postcards, jackknives, Roosevelt Bear items, pitchers, medals, and serving trays. There are so many things to be found from Teddy Roosevelt's time that many collectors just specialize in his presidency.

The last president in the so-called glory years for collectors is the portly William Howard Taft, who weighed as much as 320 pounds and was never really enthusiastic about being in the White House. Inaugurated on March 4, 1909, he remained in office until March 3, 1913. A bright, sociable man, Taft liked to travel and meet the people, a characteristic that added to the many mementos that still can be found from his presidency.

In 1912, Taft faced not only the challenge of Woodrow Wilson, but also the Bull Moose candidacy of his onetime close friend, Teddy Roosefelt. It was in this campaign that Roosevelt coined the expression of throwing his "hat in the ring," and a red-and-white bandanna made at the time reflects the theme. The Taft-Roosevelt split helped Wilson to victory as Taft departed from a role that he never enjoyed as much as he did his later service as chief justice of the Supreme Court.

In the wide wake left by Taft are many presidential collectibles. Among them are toby jugs made in Germany, plates, banks, tumblers, bandannas, bookends, canes, pipes, paperweights, baby cups, mechanical pins, postcards, watch fobs, stanhopes, tiepins, studs, ribbons, badges, and a fine assortment of celluloid buttons.

But with Taft's presidency there ended a flourishing 32-year period of campaign item productivity that was never duplicated again. Yet much of the evidence of those days remains for all to see—and for presidential memorabilia collectors to discover.

From Wilson to Reagan

Woodrow Wilson, the scholarly president who was to guide the United States through World War I while driving himself into failing health in his dedicated efforts to secure postwar peace, was inaugurated for his first term on March 4, 1913. Winning reelection in 1916, he served until March 3, 1921.

In addition to helping bring the war to a conclusion, the Wilson administration was also instrumental in producing child labor legislation, supporting the women's suffrage movement, and in pushing through antitrust legislation. But by the time of the 1920 election, with his heroic crusade for peace thwarted, and Warren Harding running for the republicans and James M. Cox for the democrats, Wilson was an ailing, disappointed man.

Rare Cox-Roosevelt jugate pocket watch, valued at $2,500

Souvenirs of the Wilson era include small china plates bearing his picture, china match holders, buttons, medals, a nutcracker, scarce toby jugs, watch fobs, watches, a metal plaque, posters, badges, jackknives, tiles, ribbons, buttonhooks, cigar cutters, pennants, and numerous other things. Wilson is a favorite of many collectors, and although a fair amount of mementos were made during his time, they are not easily found.

The team of Harding and his running mate, Calvin Coolidge, outpolled the democrats in the 1920 election, with Cox and his vice presidential partner, Franklin D. Roosevelt, losing by a plurality of nearly 7 million votes. Harding was inaugurated on March 4, 1921 and served until August 2, 1923, when he died in San Francisco at the age of 57, weary from a wave of scandals that were still being uncovered in his crony-plagued administration.

Because his days in office were comparatively short, and because not too much was produced for the 1920 campaign anyway, memorabilia from President Harding is not easily found. But there are buttons, cigars, stickpins, purses, tiles, ribbons, jackknives, banners, song sheets, medals, caps, badges, paper items, and the rare Laddie Boy dog statue—not to mention those highly coveted Cox-Roosevelt buttons from the losing side.

With Harding's death, Coolidge ascended to the presidency, taking the oath from his father, a justice of the peace, on August 3, 1923, in a middle-of-the-night oil lamp ceremony at his home in Plymouth, Vermont. Coolidge was successful when he ran for a full term in 1924. He was inaugurated on March 4, 1925 and served as America's leader during the Roaring Twenties, when everyone was fascinated with heroes like Babe Ruth and Charles A. Lindbergh. Coolidge characteristically advocated economy and the status quo while the nation drifted slowly toward a period of sharp economic decline.

Although history is rich with photos picturing "Silent Cal" wearing a variety of sober-faced expressions, quantity is lacking among the souvenirs from his years in the White House. There are buttons, a record of one of his campaign talks, badges, medals, pennants, medalets, thimbles, license plate attachments, a pottery savings bank, tiny campaign bells, and posters.

Herbert Hoover began his Depression-plagued term on March 4, 1929. While he succeeded Coolidge when the nation seemed destined for good times, everything changed within a matter of months with the crash of the stock market. Hoover pledged that he would keep the federal budget balanced, and he promised to expand spending for public works. But people were feeling the financial pinch, and Hoover was made the scapegoat for what happened. Many older Americans, in fact, still remember the Hoover presidency as the beginning of the long Depression and a time of hardship. He was defeated in his bid for reelection and left office on March 3, 1933.

Remnants of Hoover's term are paperweights, toby pitchers, pencils, badges, buttons, license attachments, inaugural souvenirs, thimbles, medalets, pins, bandannas, iron banks, postcards, spare tire covers, celluloid dice, ribbons, stickpins, handkerchiefs, and other mementos, including some highly coveted Al Smith material. Smith was the brash, likable, and well-remembered democratic loser in 1928.

Franklin D. Roosevelt, who introduced much social legislation and was to break tradition by running and winning four consecutive terms, was inaugurated for his initial victory on March 4, 1933. From that day until he died of a cerebral hemorrhage at Warm Springs, Georgia on April 12, 1945, he remained our president, having won reelection in 1936, 1940, and 1944. Not only did Roosevelt lift the spirits of the American people, his social programs (and the growing threat of war) helped put the nation back to work. Social Security and labor reforms were introduced during his years in office. He established the "good neighbor" policy in this hemisphere while also aiding our European friends in their task of meeting the growing threat emanating from Nazi Germany. He set America's great productive capacity into motion during World War II and, as that conflict began to draw to a close, was working for a strong United Nations as a means of establishing a lasting peace.

Because he guided the country through the Depression and to new heights as a world power during the war years, there naturally is an abundance of souvenirs from President Roosevelt. They include a large assortment of buttons (many of them not flattering to his disregard for tradition), badges, plates, pitchers, tumblers, license plate attachments, watch fobs, banks, pencils, posters, bandannas, statuettes, ribbons, mir-

Franklin D. Roosevelt bank

rors, lamps, serving trays, small toby jugs, mugs, neckties, paperweights, and even a cane—the latter an example of a campaign item that was in extremely poor taste, since the president was handicapped. Along with all these things, of course, are some excellent souvenirs from the men he defeated, such as Alfred Landon, Wendell Wilkie, Thomas Dewey, and others.

Harry S. Truman, the third man to serve as vice president under Roosevelt, was elevated to the presidency when Roosevelt died. He was sworn in on April 12, 1945 and, although given almost no chance of victory by the political pundits, won a full term when he upset republican Dewey after a "give 'em hell" campaign in 1948. Truman made some tough decisions as president, including the dropping of the atomic bomb, the authorization of the Berlin airlift, the firing of General Douglas McArthur, and strong action on such domestic issues as possible strikes. He also helped rebuild the war-ravaged nations and, over the years, earned the respect of the world. Today he has retained historic stature as a strong, effective president. Truman did not run in 1952 and left office when his popular successor, Dwight D. Eisenhower, was inaugurated on January 20, 1953. Except for some interesting buttons and a few other items, there are serious limits to good souvenirs from Truman's days in the White House.

$75

$50

$150

$85

$700

$700

$65

$200

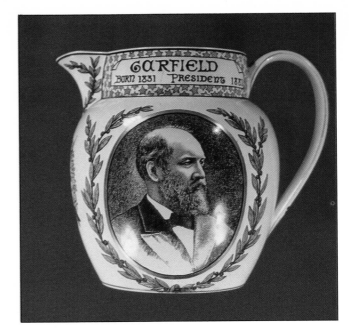

Beautifully decorated, this creamware Garfield pitcher was made by Wedgwood and carries the date of his birth and the year he took office—and was assassinated. The pitcher has become difficult to find and because of its high quality and exceptional design commands a strong price. Height, 7". **$750**

Emblazoned with patriotic decorations, this rare majolica pitcher shows James Garfield in bas-relief on each side. The spout curves upward over the wings and head of the American eagle, which rests on a red, white, and blue flag-style banner. The blue edging at the top is decorated with stars, and the handle is shaped like a twig from a tree. There are pink ribbons above and below the oval frame showing Garfield, with green leaves growing from the top and bottom of the twig handle. Registry marks appear to indicate that the pitcher was made as a memorial October 29, 1881, the month after Garfield died. Height, 6¾". **$275**

President Wilson's efforts toward peace were appreciated by many, as shown by this souvenir of his presidency. With the American flag as a backdrop, Wilson is pictured surrounded by a wooden life preserver. The top of the preserver is decorated with "U. S. A.," and the bottom says, "Our Life Preserver." Made by the American Novelty Company of Seattle, Washington. Diameter, 8¼". *$90*

Toby pitchers of Herbert Hoover and Al Smith are more frequently found than this one of Franklin D. Roosevelt; therefore, the Roosevelt one commands a higher price from collectors. It is 7" high and, though unmarked, probably was made under the Patriotic Products Association Gold Medal label. *$140*

A scarce tile picturing Warren G. Harding in color and a little leather change purse with his features embossed on metal are shown here. Harding is not identified as president on the tile, so it is probably a campaign item. An advertisement inside the little President Harding purse is for a bakery in East Stroudsburg, Pennsylvania. The tile measures 4¼" square, and the purse is 3½" wide. Tile: **$95**. Purse: **$65**

A statue of Warren Harding's famous Airedale, Laddie Boy, pictured here with presidential sheet music in the background, is a rare collectible from Harding's years in the White House. Laddie Boy was given to the president by the owner of a kennel in Toledo, Ohio and became the nation's best known pet. In fact, the dog often was at Harding's side when he greeted White House visitors, and the president liked to be photographed with him. Each morning, Laddie Boy is said to have brought President Harding his newspaper. The dog also sat in on Cabinet meetings and wore a No. 1 license when he led a "Be Kind to Animals Week" parade in Washington, DC. At the time President Harding died, children throughout the country were collecting pennies to be melted down for a national Laddie Boy statue. Beautifully made, the heavy golden Laddie Boy statue shown here is 6½" high and 6½" long. The newspaper in the dog's mouth is clearly imprinted as the (Marion) Star, Harding's old newspaper in Ohio. On the topside of the base, there's the message, "Guarding Our President," with the first letters of those three words spelling "GOP." The side of the base is inscribed "Laddie Boy," and the reverse side reads "Copyright 1921, by Elizabeth Swaffield." An extraordinarily fine piece of presidential Americana. **$650**

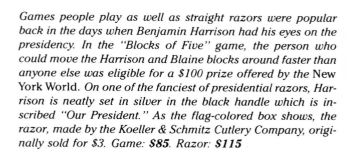

Games people play as well as straight razors were popular back in the days when Benjamin Harrison had his eyes on the presidency. In the "Blocks of Five" game, the person who could move the Harrison and Blaine blocks around faster than anyone else was eligible for a $100 prize offered by the New York World. On one of the fanciest of presidential razors, Harrison is neatly set in silver in the black handle which is inscribed "Our President." As the flag-colored box shows, the razor, made by the Koeller & Schmitz Cutlery Company, originally sold for $3. Game: **$85**. Razor: **$115**

Showcasing Taft and Sherman, this quality domed paperweight was made for the election of 1908 by the Graeser Manufacturing Company, Pittsburgh, Pennsylvania. The candidates are featured by the red, white, and blue theme that pictures an eagle atop a shield amid a background of crossed flags. A companion paperweight was made for the candidacy of Bryan and Kern. Width, 5¾". **$95**

One of the most attractive tin serving trays showing American presidents is this one of Theodore Roosevelt, made in 1903 by the Meek & Beach Company of Coshocton, Ohio. The 16½" by 13½" tray has a floral border, and the center pictures Roosevelt in the formal, dignified pose made famous in the painting by John S. Sargent. Roosevelt also is portrayed in the floral border as a cowboy and Rough Rider. The Sargent painting was used on the tray through the permission of Collier's Weekly and undoubtedly helped promote Roosevelt's cause in the 1904 election. An advertisement on the back shows that this particular tray was distributed through the St. Paul Pioneer Press, the "oldest and best newspaper in the northwest." Other business firms also used the trays as gifts for customers. **$130**

Nine-inch campaign "buttons" were used on little stands that some store owners placed in their windows to promote the candidacy of Richard Nixon in his losing race against John F. Kennedy in 1960. Nixon's youthful face appears in the center of a red, white, and blue shield. **$40**

Several different versions of this attractive ribbon appeared during the 1896 presidential election. This one was made for the Sons of Soldiers Marching Club to help promote the candidacy of William McKinley, who had served with honor during the Civil War before entering politics. With eagle and fringe attachment, the ribbon showing McKinley and Garret Hobart is 8¼" long. **$60**

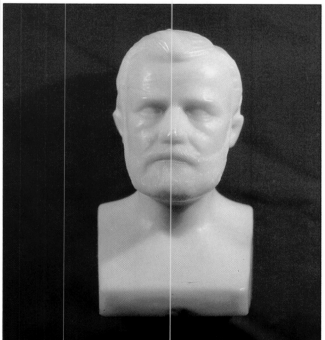

Ulysses S. Grant was winding up a disappointing presidency in 1876, the year that the nation celebrated its Centennial. As a result, mementos that were made for that observance included Grant, as demonstrated by this milk-glass bust made by Gillinder & Sons on the Centennial grounds in Philadelphia. The Grant statuette is harder to find than the Lincoln bust, also made by Gillinder, and is highly regarded by presidential collectors because it was made while Grant was in office. Well-sculptured, the Grant bust is 5¾" high and can also be found in clear glass with an acid finish. **$450**

From the Golden Age of Buttons

$60 $200 $350 $1,100

$80 $125 $250 $60 $90

$200 $240 $140 $65 $75

$125 $90 $250 $90 $125

$150 $250 $200 $70 $70

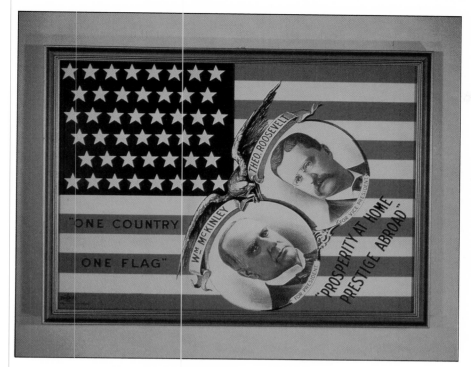

Old Glory proved to be an effective campaign poster for McKinley in 1900 as this one, bearing the theme "One Country, One Flag" clearly shows. McKinley and his vigorous running mate, Theodore Roosevelt, are attractively illustrated, along with the slogan, "Prosperity at Home, Prestige Abroad." It was a time when the U.S. was reaching out to become a world power. The union label is proudly displayed on this poster by "Edwards, Deutsch & Heitmann, Litho, Chicago." The framed poster measures 24⅞" by 18⅜".
$350

One of the most handsome presidential platters is this beauty, picturing in full color the White House, the coats of arms of eight states (Pennsylvania, New York, California, Virginia, Illinois, Ohio, Missouri, and Texas) and medallions of ten presidents—the last being William McKinley. Presidents shown include Washington, Jefferson, Monroe, Jackson, Lincoln, Grant, Garfield, Cleveland, Benjamin Harrison, and McKinley. The colored White House transfer image is signed "Palm, Fechyeler & Co.," and the back of the platter is marked "La Francaise Porcelain." Length, 13¾". Width, 10⅝". **$300**

William Howard Taft and his vice presidential candidate, James Schoolcraft Sherman, are pictured on this beautiful full-color "Grand Old Party Standard Bearers" tin plate made in 1908 by the Meek Company of Coshocton, Ohio. Enhanced by gorgeous color and handsome design, the plate shows all republicans who carried the GOP banner from 1856 to 1908 and is decorated with shields, the American flag, and the White House. It still appears on the market frequently, and, because of its quality and historic excellence, it ranks as a bargain. Diameter, 9½". **$90**

William Jennings Bryan and Adlai Stevenson ran as the democratic team in the 1900 election and are shown on this jugate tin serving tray copyrighted by the Charles W. Shonk Company, lithographers in Chicago. Miss Liberty and two shields, plus a background of stars, add political flavor to the tray. Diameter, 12". **$185**

Benjamin Harrison and Levi Morton are supported in this brightly colored silk flag bandanna made for the election in 1888. It was patented June 28, 1888, and was made by A. S. Rosenthal & Company, New York. Slogans on the bandanna, which measures 19" by 20", call for "Pensions for Soldiers," "Aid for Free Schools," and "Protection vs. Free Trade." **$110**

Ulysses S. Grant's well-executed bas-relief features make this a particularly impressive green jasperware wall plaque. Great detail can be found in the face, eyes, hair, and uniform, reflecting the artistry of the designer. The plaque measures 7". **$95**

Collapsible paper campaign lanterns were made with colorful graphics for the 1888 election in which Benjamin Harrison defeated Grover Cleveland. Both candidates are shown here along with patriotic symbols designed to stir the enthusiasm of the voters. Made with a wire and wood frame, the lanterns were produced by the Sprague and French firm of Norwalk, Ohio. Each: $225

When it comes to political campaign umbrellas, it's hard to beat the dramatic flair shown in those that were made in 1900, when William McKinley sought reelection with his running mate, Theodore Roosevelt. When these are found in good condition, buyers are always available. $300

Small bisque figures of Grover Cleveland and Benjamin Harrison, each draped in a flag, dangle from a tiny wooden scale in this amusing and rare artifact from the 1888 election. We aren't sure whether it's designed to show that one is a lightweight or the other is a heavyweight. Either way, it's a delightful remnant of our great political history. The scale is 5½" long. $850

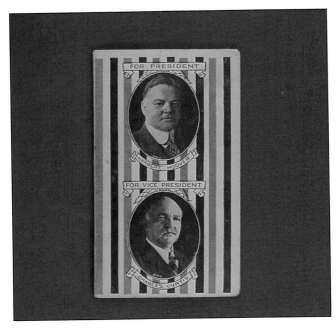

Used as a campaign item to help voters "stick to the Republican Party," this colorful little package of needles from the 1928 election today is a popular memento among political collectors. The cover shows Herbert Hoover and his vice presidential mate, Charles Curtis, and the back cover pictures an elephant wearing the GOP banner along with the wording, "Work and Vote for the Republican Party and Prosperity." The needles are inside the package, which also carries the biographies of the two GOP candidates. Size: 2¾" by 4¾". **$20**

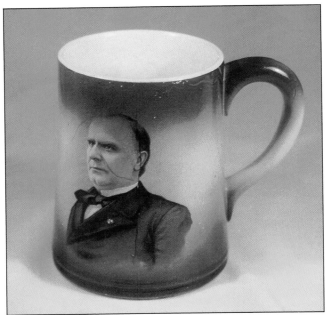

A good color portrait appears on this scarce green mug made to make the voters conscious of the abilities of William McKinley. The mug, which stands nearly 5" high, is especially popular with presidential collectors who prefer glass and china. **$100**

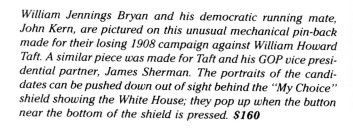

William Jennings Bryan and his democratic running mate, John Kern, are pictured on this unusual mechanical pin-back made for their losing 1908 campaign against William Howard Taft. A similar piece was made for Taft and his GOP vice presidential partner, James Sherman. The portraits of the candidates can be pushed down out of sight behind the "My Choice" shield showing the White House; they pop up when the button near the bottom of the shield is pressed. **$160**

"Honest Old Abe" is the way Abraham Lincoln is described on this scarce red campaign ribbon made for the 1860 election. Lincoln, who didn't have a beard at that time, ran with Hannibal Hamlin as his vice presidential mate. The ribbon is 7" long by 2" wide. **$675**

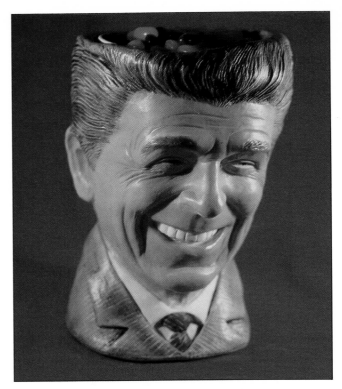

A jellybean holder or planter made to remind America that President Ronald Reagan has a sweet tooth. The Reagan piece has the markings of Accents Unlimited Incorporated and "Melville Tiess 1981." Sold in plaster shops around the country, painted or plain. Height, 9¼". Painted, **$25**

There's a realistic look to this toby honoring Dwight Eisenhower for his many military achievements. Eisenhower is wearing his five-star shirt and appears as most Americans remember him—around the time that World War II came to an end. Good color and a fine collectible. Marked "Barrington" on the base. Height, 7¼". **$100**

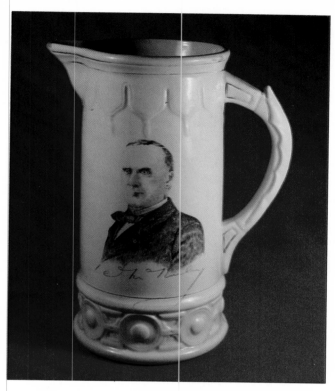

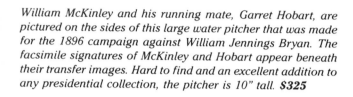

William McKinley and his running mate, Garret Hobart, are pictured on the sides of this large water pitcher that was made for the 1896 campaign against William Jennings Bryan. The facsimile signatures of McKinley and Hobart appear beneath their transfer images. Hard to find and an excellent addition to any presidential collection, the pitcher is 10" tall. **$325**

William McKinley is shown in bas-relief on this unusual German beer stein. The president's image is lifelike, with realistic features and coloring. The German moldmaker misspelled McKinley's name however, making it "MacKinley." The error only adds interest to this desirable presidential item. It is 5¾" high. **$110**

Beautifully sewn in an imaginative and probably unique flag design, this large and colorful textile captures the essence of Franklin Roosevelt's 1932 campaign when his running mate was John Nance Garner. The textile is comprised of 37 separate strips bearing the slogans "Roosevelt," and "Repeal 18th Amendment," all in color and assembled in the form of the American flag. Such strips come on the market occasionally as singles, but the dedicated work of some Roosevelt admirer has made this into an outstanding souvenir of the 1932 presidential election. Framed, it measures 54" by 32½". **$850**

"Bob" La Follette's 1924 presidential candidacy was given a boost on this cigar box, copyrighted in 1923 by a Madison, Wisconsin cigar seller, George Wiese. La Follette's face also appears in full color on the side of the box. The "Governor" cigars sold for "10¢ straight." **$22**

An old campaign button recalls Camelot

An American hero in World War II, Eisenhower served two full terms in the White House at a time when the United States was at the peak of its power as a nation. He suffered a heart attack in 1955, yet ran for a second term in 1956 and polled more votes than he did in his first election. There were minor recessions and heightened tensions with the Soviet Union during the Eisenhower years, but the Korean War was ended and the country remained strong.

There are many souvenirs of the Eisenhower presidency, including ceramic toby mugs of the president and first lady, Mamie, along with such mementos as buttons, cigarette lighters, bandannas, jewelry, ribbons, cigarettes, salt and pepper shakers, bubble gum cigars, a liquor bottle, plates, ties, hats, badges, medals, bumper attachments, rulers, banners, and numerous paper items.

John F. Kennedy, a handsome, 43-year-old democrat, defeated republican Richard Nixon, who had served as vice president under Eisenhower in the extremely close 1960 election. Kennedy had to overcome the political handicaps of being young and being Roman Catholic. Nationally televised debates with Nixon helped him achieve those objectives, and he went on to win the election.

After a brilliant inaugural address on January 20, 1961, President Kennedy embarked upon a strong civil rights policy, created the Peace Corps, pledged the country to an outstanding space program de-

signed to land man on the moon, and forced the Russians to back down during the dangerous Cuban missile crisis of 1962. His difficulties were a disastrous Bay of Pigs invasion in Cuba and his questionable Vietnam War policies. The nation was thrown into a period of deep grief when the young president was assassinated in Dallas by Lee Harvey Oswald on November 22, 1963.

Recalling the Kennedy years for collectors are such mementos as paperweights, plaster busts, salt and pepper shakers, buttons, ribbons, tumblers, cigars, dolls, hats, jewelry, license plate attachments, medals, banners, plates, creamers, and many paper souvenirs. As in the case of Lincoln, Garfield, and McKinley, many memorial items were manufactured and are still being turned out today.

Taking the oath of office on the Day of Kennedy's death, Lyndon B. Johnson charted a course that would carry out the civil rights hopes of his predecessor—and history shows that in that regard he did an excellent job. Voters elected him to a complete term by an overwhelming margin in 1964, when he defeated republican Senator Barry Goldwater. Strong on social reforms, Johnson sought to establish the "Great Society" and also continued enthusiastic support for the American space program. But increasing involvement in the Vietnam War splintered the nation, and this factionalism shattered whatever dreams Johnson may have had of seeking reelection. In March 1968 he announced that he would not run for another term. Three months later, Senator Robert Kennedy, the brother of President Kennedy, was assassinated in Los Angeles after an encouraging triumph in the California presidential primary. The democratic nomination during that turbulent year went to Johnson's vice president, Hubert H. Humphrey, after a violence-marred party convention in Chicago. Humphrey was narrowly defeated in the November election by republican Richard M. Nixon, who had staged what many regarded as an impressive political comeback.

Souvenirs from the Johnson years include cups and saucers, buttons, badges, ashtrays, belt buckles, plates, dolls, posters, jewelry, hats, pennants, ribbons, license plate attachments, bubble gum cigars, trays, cloth patches, pitchers, teapots, a clock, creamers, and a variety of other items.

Nixon was inaugurated on January 20, 1969, with Spiro Agnew as his vice president. On July 20 that year, astronauts Neil Armstrong and Edwin Aldrin landed on the moon, giving the United States new prestige in space and a boost for the Nixon presidency. However, great unrest continued over Nixon's Vietnam War policies that extended the conflict into Cambodia and Laos. This feeling was heightened on May 1, 1970, when four students at Kent State University in Ohio were killed by guardsmen during a demonstration against the war. The president kept withdrawing American troops from Vietnam, seeking "peace with honor," while also opening important negotiations with China.

But other things also were happening in the Nixon administration. On June 17, 1972, arrests were made and a full investigation was promised after a break-in at the Democratic National Committee Headquarters in the Watergate complex in Washington. Later that year President Nixon was reelected, and in January 1973 a cease-fire was signed to end the Vietnam War. But through persistent reporting in the *Washington Post,* and demands by the press throughout the nation for an explanation of the Watergate episode, evidence began to mount that the president was engaged in a cover-up. There were calls for the impeachment of Nixon, and the Watergate scandal overshadowed whatever else the administration was doing. Vice President Agnew resigned in October 1973 on tax evasion charges, and his appointed successor was Gerald R. Ford. Ultimately, Nixon aides were implicated in the Watergate break-in, and as a result of the truth revealed in tapes of conversations that had been held in the president's office, Nixon also was forced to resign. On August 9, 1974, he left the White House.

Although the scandal associated with President Nixon does not make him a favorite of some collectors, his years as the nation's leader certainly were historic. He was the first president to resign, and that alone would qualify him as an unusually collectible chief executive.

Among souvenirs from the Nixon presidency are plates, salt and pepper shakers, buttons, badges, jewelry, combs, playing cards, a Watergate pitcher, clickers, bubble gum cigars, cigarette lighters, hats, and a wide array of ephemera.

With Nixon having departed in dishonor, Gerald Ford, by virtue of the 25th Amendment, became president of the United States on August 9, 1974. On August 20, he nominated Nelson Rockefeller to be his vice president and, following hearings, Rockefeller was sworn in on December 19, 1974. For the first time in history, the country had both a president and a vice president who had not been elected to their respective offices.

During his comparatively short time in the White House, President Ford reestablished trust in the nation's highest office although he was severely criticized for granting Nixon an unconditional pardon. He offered amnesty to young Americans who had dodged the draft as well as to those who had deserted from the military. President Ford also played a major role in the planning for the nation's great Bicentennial celebration, and he sought to rally Congress and the people to fight rising inflation. In addition, he ordered the evacuation of the last remaining Americans in Vietnam and authorized an investigation into the domestic operations of the Central Intelligence Agency.

This was not enough to assure him of election to the office he held, however, and in the campaign of 1976 voters—apparently wanting to shake free of all ties with the former Nixon administration—elected Jimmy Carter, a peanut farmer from Georgia.

Souvenirs of Ford's presidency are in comparatively short supply, but they include plates, mugs, buttons, paperweights, badges, and paper collectibles. As time places more distance between the healing months of dedicated service that Ford gave to the nation, there will be a growing appreciation for memorabilia from his brief administration. And in the years ahead, that should give them added value.

Jimmy Carter was inaugurated on January 20, 1977, as an "outsider" with no crippling ties to the Washington establishment. He had made hundreds of promises in his campaign—pledging welfare reforms, cuts in the bureaucracy, and a balanced budget. But his performance did not live up to the hopes of the people, and he fell steadily in national polls. Carter was plagued by energy problems, inflation, unemployment, an inadequate working relationship with Congress, and divisions within the Democratic Party (particularly from those who began to look favorably upon a run for the presidency by Senator Edward Kennedy). Critics of President Carter became more vocal when American citizens were taken captive in Iran and held there for 444 days, despite efforts of the United States government during all that time to set them free.

Among Carter's best achievements were his bid to assure peace for the Mideast by bringing together Israel's Menachem Begin and Egypt's Anwar Sadat and his strengthening of the bonds between China and the United States. He also was regarded as the world's leading spokesman for human rights. Carter sought reelection in 1980, but the national mood was for change—in the person of a former movie actor, Ronald W. Reagan, who scored an impressive election victory.

Many items that mark the presidency of Jimmy Carter were made in the form of a peanut—mugs, buttons, canes, jewelry, and vases, for example. But there were also plates, paperweights, ribbons, watches, umbrellas, badges, peanut holders (or flowerpots), and a good supply of paper and other collectibles.

President Reagan, who at age 69 was the oldest man ever elected to the White House, was inaugurated on January 20, 1981. He pledged a strong America and an economic strategy that would drive down inflation and make progress in balancing the federal budget. Even though many feared cutbacks in social programs that had grown since the days of Franklin Roosevelt, thousands of democrats who had been disappointed by President Carter gave Reagan their support.

However, President Reagan's first days in office were marred by an attack on his life. On March 30,

Lights, music for 1984 Reagan button

1981, John Hinckley, Jr., a 25-year-old drifter, shot Reagan outside the Washington Hilton. Following his recovery from a chest wound, the president vigorously demonstrated his political skills in winning bipartisan backing for many of his key programs. President Reagan was easily reelected in 1984, defeating democrat Walter Mondale and his vice presidential running mate, Geraldine Ferraro, who had hoped to become the country's first woman vice president. Although he restored the United States to military strength, revived the spirit of patriotism, and brought inflation under control, Reagan's second term had its problems. He was in frequent conflict with a Congress controlled by the opposition party as he urged spending restraints and welfare reforms, saying in 1988 that the federal budget process "needs a drastic overhaul." But the most criticism he faced came from the prolonged Iran-Contra investigation regarding the shipment of military aid to Iran and funds for "freedom fighters" in Nicaragua. In the final months of his second term, President Reagan pledged that he would continue to seek "what is best for America."

The Reagan presidency has provided collectors with an interesting assortment of souvenirs, including such items as buttons, umbrellas, paperweights, old movie posters, an elaborately topped "Ron Jar" jellybean holder, a paper doll cutout book, a ceramic jellybean White House, a plaster flowerpot holder (also used for jellybeans), badges, ribbons, tumblers, textiles, a toby jug, iron banks, a jugate bottle and more, including some rather fancy inaugural mementos.

And today, as President Reagan prepares to bid farewell after two eventful terms in the White House, collectors all across the land are busier than ever—hunting for souvenirs from those who desire to be his successor.

The Presidential Plates of P. J. Jacobus

For decades, collectors of presidential memorabilia, as well as glass historians everywhere, have recognized the four Classic Pattern portrait plates made for the election of 1884 as the zenith in historic glass perfection.

Pictured on the 11-inch plates are the candidates for president and vice president—democrats Grover Cleveland and Thomas A. Hendricks, and republicans James G. Blaine and John A. Logan. Their center portraits are framed within a rim of pointed Gothic panels that feature the familiar daisy-and-button pattern and arches that display a leaf design.

But it's the artistic, lifelike detail of the portraits themselves, set against a lightly stippled and frosted background, that makes the plates so unusual. No other images in glass equal these, not even the skillfully made busts of George Washington, Abraham Lincoln, Ulysses S. Grant, and Benjamin Franklin produced in Philadelphia by Gillinder & Sons during the 1876 Centennial, nor the handsome jugate trays of Cleveland and Hendricks and Blaine and Logan, that also were made for the 1884 campaign, nor the similar (but without handles) jugate trays that boosted the candidacies of Cleveland and Allen Thurman and Benjamin Harrison and Levi Morton, for the campaign of 1888. The reason the quality is so high in all these pieces is that they were all created by the same man—a greatly esteemed but little-known moldmaker named Philip J. Jacobus.

For years there have been only vague published references to Jacobus as a gifted German moldmaker who was employed by the Gillinder firm. He has therefore remained an elusive figure for glass researchers, and, until now, little has been known about Jacobus the man.

Born in Kreuznach, Prussia, on May 20, 1844, Jacobus came to this country when he was just a boy, in 1851. An older brother, Peter H. Jacobus, who had come to the United States earlier, operated a steel en-

P. J. Jacobus and his wife

graving and diemaking business at Third and Chestnut streets in Philadelphia. That's where Philip received his early training and developed his skills as a moldmaker. Old wax letter-seals designed by the Jacobus brothers occasionally still can be found.

When the Civil War began, Peter Jacobus, who had been an officer in the Prussian army, organized a company of Union volunteers. Commissioned a captain, he entered active service and left young Philip, a teenager, in charge of the business. Much of the money from the work that Philip did was sent to aid the Union troops. That financial drain contributed to problems that led to the closing of the engraving firm. Moreover, Peter Jacobus was wounded in the war, received a pension, and never sought to return to his craft.

But by war's end, Philip had become highly proficient as a steel engraver as well as a diesinker and moldmaker. He had begun to make steel stamps and dies for other companies and, in addition, engraved printing plates for bonds and securities. At one time, the United States government sought his talents for the Philadelphia Mint. Philip Jacobus declined, not wanting to work in such confinement. "It's too much like being in prison," he said.

An artist of great curiosity, Jacobus, a thin, bespectacled man with a shaggy handlebar mustache and goatee, kept improving his techniques. He studied many books on the human form and was fascinated as well by the graceful beauty of animals. He was always observing details that helped bring maximum reality to his work. He made molds for desk sets, commemorative medals, and steel statues of birds and dogs. One decorative desk set he is known to have made features animals in a wooded hunting scene. He is credited with being the moldmaker for Gillinder's fine Westward Ho and Lion pattern glass, and his penchant for reality also may be reflected in precise bear-paw handles on the Washington bread trays in the Centennial pattern.

Jacobus, who married and had four children, freelanced his moldmaking talents. He even set up workshops in the two homes in which he lived in Philadelphia, one located at Twelfth and York streets and the other at 1133 W. Erie Avenue. They were simple workshops, with just a bench and some tools, but they provided a place for him to toil on a variety of assignments that kept him busy and earning a living.

Wesley I. Slagle of Philadelphia, a great-grandson of the moldmaker, told me that Jacobus made molds for the expositions that were held in Chicago in 1893 and in St. Louis in 1904. Slagle also owns a signed plate from the St. Louis Exposition. In addition, he has two beer mugs decorated with the images of early baseball players. Both of the baseball mugs have cooling cracks, however, since they are believed to be the first examples poured, revealing a production flaw.

Along with his talents as a moldmaker, Jacobus also enjoyed painting. He found creative satisfaction in painting mountain scenes in clamshells, emphasizing the same attention to detail that he displayed in sculpting molds for glass.

But of all the objects he may have created or beautified, Jacobus, who, after suffering a stroke, died on January 23, 1910 at the age of 65, is best remembered today for the molds he designed for the Gillinder firm. The company gained world recognition during the 1876 Centennial by setting up a complete glassmaking operation right on the grounds in Philadelphia. It was at that time that Jacobus fashioned the fine acid-finish busts of Washington, Lincoln, and Grant in both clear and milk glass that presidential collectors now seek.

Yet, in the author's opinion, the peak of his moldmaking artistry is exemplified in the Classic Pattern plates that Jacobus, in collaboration with John Putnam, made for the 1884 election. These were extraordinary molds of Cleveland, Hendricks, Blaine, and Logan, showing details in the hair and eyebrows, facial expressions, sensitivity in the eyes, lines and wrinkles in the skin, and clothing so carefully copied that if colored it would look like real cloth. They capture in beautiful clear-frosted glass a political campaign that often was characterized by the cartoonists of the day and by the contemporary press as a period of mudslinging. Jacobus apparently didn't see the campaign with such limited vision. He saw four interesting faces and four human beings—and that's what he duplicated for history, even better than a camera could have done.

Little wonder then, after putting so much of himself into each work of art, that he signed the Hendricks and Blaine plates in his characteristic way, "P. J. Jacobus, scul."

Time has shown that Jacobus was indeed much more than a moldmaker.

Presidential Memorabilia
with Prices

George Washington
1789–1797

George Washington is shown in color in this reverse painting on glass which appears on a little patch box dating from the 1840s. The glass is bordered by gold paper trim, and beneath the cover is a mirror. The sides of the box are made to look like pages in a closed book. On the reverse side of the 2¾" × 1¾" glass-covered box is the reminder, "Forget Me Not." $425

George Washington was well remembered at the time of the 1876 Centennial, and this china mug with American flags, eagle, and Washington's framed countenance is a good example. Made by W. T. Copeland & Sons for J. M. Shaw & Company of New York, such mugs and cups were sold as Centennial souvenirs. Washington's name and "1776" are on one side. The other side reads, "A Memorial of the Centennial, 1876." The cup measures 3" high. On some of the mugs and cups, the illustration is in color. $90

One of the earliest ribbons issued as a tribute to our nation's first president, this one was circulated by the Washington Benevolent Society. The "pro patria" at the top honors Washington as a patriot, while the eagle symbol appears over the oval that features a rather crude likeness of the president. "Washington Benevolent Society" is listed below. The ribbon is 6½" long × 2¼" wide. $250

Clothing buttons made for the presidency of George Washington have become rare collectibles today. Those shown here bear the initials "GW" in the center and carry the wording, "Long Live the President." Over the years, Washington buttons have been reproduced, so buyers must learn to distinguish the old from those that were manufactured later. As we approach the bicentennial of Washington's inauguration, the original clothing buttons can be expected to increase in value. (L) $650; (C) $950; (R) $1,200

George and Martha Washington appear as tintypes on this silver-plated belt buckle sold at the time of the Centennial in 1876. The buckle is 2⅛" high × 3¼" wide. A good Americana piece. $90

"First in war, first in peace, and first in the hearts of his countrymen." This familiar quotation, associated with George Washington, appeared on bread plates honoring our first president at the time of the 1876 Centennial. This one shows the image of Washington frosted, but the heavy tray also was made in all-clear and all-frosted glass. The bearpaw handles are embossed "Centennial" and carry the 1776 and 1876 dates. Made by Gillinder & Sons of Philadelphia; length, 12". $130

The Houdon bust of George Washington is highlighted in this medallion paperweight made by Gillinder & Sons of Philadelphia for the 1876 Centennial. The sides, upper edging and intaglio image of Washington are acid-treated to contribute to the impressive contrast. Diameter, 3"; height, 1". An excellent paperweight. $160

The special place that George Washington will always have in American history is reflected on this plate, made for the 1876 Centennial. The flags are in color, and the border of the 6" plate is embossed with the words, "Our Union Forever" and "Centennial." $100

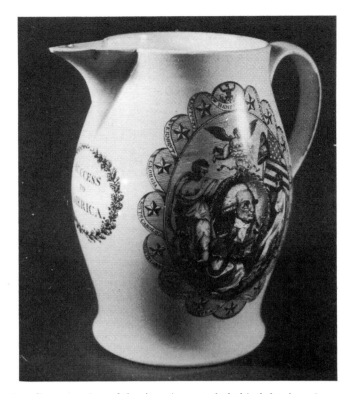

Americans always have been fascinated by things associated with our first president. At the time of the nation's Centennial celebration in 1876, Washington's carriage was on display; here it's pictured on a stereo card sold by the Centennial Photographic Company. The card is 7 × 4¼". **$10**

Owning a Liverpool pitcher bearing the image of George Washington is a challenging goal for any presidential collector. The one pictured here, circa 1800, shows our first president surrounded by the symbols of Liberty in a pose that reflects the adoration bestowed upon him by a young nation. The scene is decorated with a star border along with the names of 15 states. Under the spout of the pitcher, which stands 7" high, is a wreath enclosing the words "Success to America." On the reverse is a fierce version of the American eagle behind the American shield. A superior relic, this would be a jewel in any collection. **$1,800**

John Adams
1797–1801

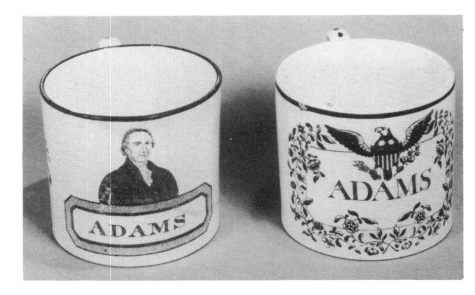

Little ceramic mugs were made to honor the presidency of John Adams. His image and his name appear on one, while the other emphasizes the Adams name within a floral border topped by the American eagle. The mugs probably were made before 1820; height, 2½". Picture mug **$1,500**; Eagle mug **$950**

John Adams is shown in this gold-and-black silhouette in glass, with his name written in signature form within the bottom border; it was probably made before 1820. The wooden frame is 7⅛" × 8⅛". **$250**

Thomas Jefferson
1801–1809

One of the presidential rarities in the country today is this silver Thomas Jefferson inauguration medal, dated 1801 and designed by diesinker John Reich. After seeing the medal, Jefferson called Reich "an artist . . . who appears to be equal to any in the world." Surrounding the bust is the wording "Th: Jefferson President of the U.S. 4 March 1801." The medal may have been the first commemorative struck at the mint. Few of these are known to exist. **$14,000**

Buildings made for the World's Fair in St. Louis in 1904 are featured on the border of this blue-and-white plate which honors President Thomas Jefferson, "Father of the Louisiana Purchase." The Rowland and Marsellus Company plate was designed and imported by Barr's of St. Louis for the World's Fair; diameter, 10". **$65**

51

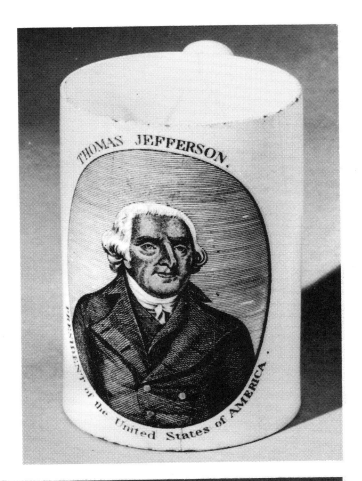

A Liverpool mug bearing a rather heavy-handed transfer image of Thomas Jefferson identifies him as "President of the United States of America." This same transfer appears on other items, including a Liverpool pitcher. Collectors need not worry too much about cracks when these types of presidential relics come along. Rare. **$1,500**

Thomas Jefferson's inaugural address is carried on the second page of this March 16, 1801, edition of the Boston Gazette. A man of immense ability, Jefferson displayed his humility when he remarked that he had "a sincere consciousness that the task is above my talents." He also asked members of Congress for their guidance and support. The same issue contains references to John Hancock, James Madison, and others of early prominence. The paper is tabloid size. **$75**

James Madison
1809–1817

An old silhouette, painted on glass in gold and decorated with black for details, honors President James Madison. This is a companion silhouette to the one picturing John Adams, with the name shown in signature form in the gold rectangle below the profile of Madison. The wooden frame is 7⅛" × 8⅛".
$250

James Monroe
1817–1825

The potters misspelled the name of President James Monroe when they made this little 2½" mug featuring a floral and eagle design. The error adds to the interest and shows that English craftsmen were more attuned to selling than to accuracy in producing presidential souvenirs for the American market. Similar to one of the mugs made for John Adams. Scarce. ***$950***

John Quincy Adams
1825–1829

A picture of John Quincy Adams adorns the inside lid of this little sewing box that was made as a campaign item for the election of 1824. The sides are decorated in rainbow colors, and the top and bottom edges feature gold paper trim. The tops of these boxes carried such slogans as "Adams Forever" and "Victory for Adams." Excellent presidential relics. Rare. **$1,250**

John Quincy Adams was among the early presidents pictured in the colored lithographs of N. Currier. Here, he's shown behind glass in an old wooden frame of the period that measures 14¼" X 16¼". Adams is identified as the "6th President of the United States." There were many presidential prints made by N. Currier and Currier & Ives, and all are growing in value. **$120**

Andrew Jackson
1829–1837

Jackson's conflict with the federal bank led to hard-times tokens that portrayed him as dictatorial and irresponsible about the nation's economy. This well-worn token is an example. On this side of the token, Jackson is supposedly saying "I take the responsibility," and on the reverse is the comment,

"The Constitution as I understand it." **$18** (in condition shown)

Two presidential numismatic items from the days of Andrew Jackson are shown. The larger one circulated at the time of his 1828 campaign against John Quincy Adams; the other was used in 1832 when he defeated Henry Clay. Other tokens and medalets were also made. Since prices vary, collectors should study numismatics to become familiar with the field. 1828 **$500**; 1832 **$175**

Andrew Jackson is pictured as "The Hero of New Orleans" on this handsome luster pitcher that probably served as a campaign item back in 1828. Such pieces are rare and, like this one from the Smithsonian Institution, often wind up in a museum—or on display in the home of a lucky collector. **$1,300**

One of the outstanding silhouettists of all time, William Henry Brown, a native of Charleston, South Carolina, cut this impressive silhouette of Andrew Jackson from life, and it appeared in his book in 1845. That was the year that Jackson died. However, the silhouette shows a trim Jackson, with flowing white hair; it probably was cut by Brown a year or two earlier. Brown's book, which included silhouettes of other famous poltical figures of that era, was published by E. B. and C. C. Kellogg. The Jackson silhouette, not including the frame, is 13¼" deep × 10" wide. **$150**

This Andrew Jackson portrait flask, made by the Keene Glass Works of New Hampshire in 1828 for his campaign against John Quincy Adams, is 6¾" high and dark olive green in color. Above his embossed image is the name "JACKSON," and a portrait of Washington is on the other side. Only five of our presidents are pictured on the early flasks—Washington, John Quincy Adams, Jackson, William H. Harrison, and Zachary Taylor. Eleven different molds were used for the Jackson flasks. All are scarce. **$375**

Well-worn silks that carry the printed inaugural address delivered by Andrew Jackson continue to turn up from time to time. When framed to protect the delicacy of the silk, they make fine keepsakes from the days of our seventh president. Size: 10⅜" wide × 13" high. **$450**

Martin Van Buren
1837–1841

This Martin Van Buren medalet is from the 1840 campaign, and on the reverse it shows a scale weighing the Whig and Democratic parties. The Whigs are shown to be the lightweights. The wording on the scale side reads, "Weighed in the balance & found wanting." **$35** (in good condition)

The great Daniel Webster signed and mailed this letter when he was serving in the United States Senate. Striking in appearance, Webster was among the most gifted leaders and orators this country ever produced. Yet even though he was a Whig presidential candidate in 1836, the presidency always eluded him. The reverse side of the letter shown carries Webster's black seal, with the initials "DW." Webster is pictured next to the letter, which is 5¼" × 3" in size. **$150**

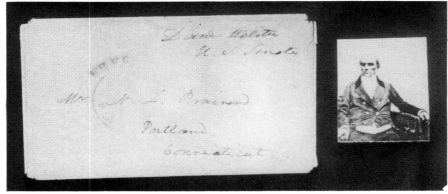

William Henry Harrison
1841

A rare ribbon from the days of Martin Van Buren also pictures Washington, Jefferson, and Jackson. The well-decorated presidential artifact is 7½" long × 2½" wide. A highly desirable memento, it captures the political drama of an interesting era. **$1,400**

"Harrison and Reform" was one of the slogans in the lively 1840 campaign when the backers of General Harrison went all out to get their man elected. This beautiful copper luster pitcher, which shows the candidate, was made for the campaign. With its graceful design, the pitcher is a rarity that any presidential collector would treasure. **$1,300**

Although he died after only one month in office, William H. Harrison today is remembered by an enormous amount of interesting memorabilia. This item is a cup plate showing Harrison and listing the date of his birth while also carrying the identification "President" and the year, "1841." The plate was made by the Boston & Sandwich Glass Factory. Harrison was the first president to die while serving in the White House. The diameter of the plate is 3½". **$50**

The log cabin theme and military background were emphasized in this attractive campaign ribbon made for William H. Harrison in his 1840 race against Martin Van Buren. The ribbon is 6½" long × 2½" wide. **$185**

A campaign clothing button picturing a log cabin and the slogan "Harrison and Reform" appears at left along with two Harrison campaign medalets. There is a variety of these items dating back to the 1840 race between Harrison and Van Buren and, because of the abundance, most have remained "good buys" for the collector. Wear as well as scarcity help determine prices on such items. Clothing button **$35**; Center medalet **$30**; Medalet on right **$18**

Mourning ribbons for an incumbent president were made for the first time with the death of William Henry Harrison, who died April 4, 1841 after being in office for only a month. This one shows the American eagle holding an oval picture of Harrison, while flags are draped below. The ribbon is appropriately trimmed in black. It is 8¼" long × 3⅛" wide. **$90**

William H. Harrison's log cabin and barrel of hard cider campaign touched off the production of Columbian Star tableware, decorated with a log cabin and a cider barrel in a tranquil rural setting. This is a handleless cup, but there also are many other attractive pieces. China made for the Harrison campaign came in several colors, and some pieces were adorned with the medallion likeness of Harrison. The cup shown here is 2¼" high. **$75**

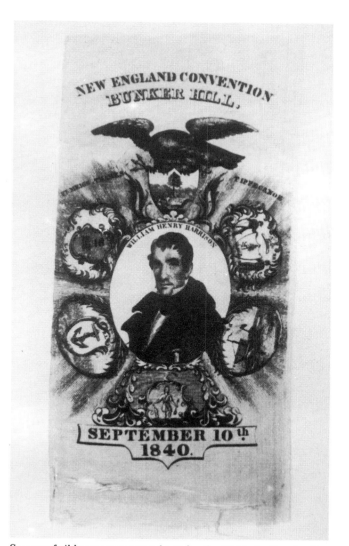

Scores of ribbons were turned out for the 1840 election for the Whig candidacy of William H. Harrison. This one captures a rather vigorous-looking Harrison in the center spotlight, even though he was 68 and destined to die just seven months later. The ribbon is 6½" × 3". **$150**

The banner that waves across the American flag on this short (2¼" × 3½") red ribbon urges the voters of 1840 to support the Whig candidates, Harrison and Tyler. A valid reminder of our political past. **$60**

John Tyler
1841–1845

Cut from life while John Tyler occupied the White House, this silhouette by William Henry Brown provides us with an excellent physical impression of our tenth president. The silhouette appeared in Brown's book, published while Tyler was president. The book later was republished since a great part of the original edition was destroyed by fire. Tyler's silhouette was one of 27 famous men of that era who were pictured in the book. Brown's work often is compared to that of August Edouart, regarded as best silhouettist ever. This likeness of Tyler is treasured by presidential collectors who realize that finding anything at all from his years in office is difficult. Size: 13¼" × 10". **$150**

Because he was the first of our presidents to gain office as a result of the death of an incumbent, John Tyler, who succeeded William H. Harrison, poses a challenge for those seeking Tyler collectibles. Few items were made, other than those that mentioned his name and were turned out for Harrison's campaign. That's why this presidential ribbon is a highly desired piece. Believed to be made in 1841, it shows a good likeness of President Tyler and carries a quotation that reflects his strong character. It is 6½" long × 3" wide. **$1,000**

Interesting graphics characterize this democratic national badge for James K. Polk and his running mate, George M. Dallas. The ribbon appeared during the campaign of 1844. Scarce. **$700**

Henry Clay is described as the "Protector of American Industry" on this well-illustrated campaign ribbon. The Clay campaign of 1844 stressed his support for American industry in many ways, but the people seemed more in tune with the expansionist ideas of Polk. The ribbon is 7½" long. **$170**

"Clear the Way for Democracy," says the banner above the eagle on this rare ribbon picturing James K. Polk. Beneath Polk's picture is a quotation from Jackson that says, "Let Polk and Dallas be the watchword and countersign and victory is certain." An excellent ribbon from a troubled time in our nation's history, it measures 6¾" long × 3" wide. **$900**

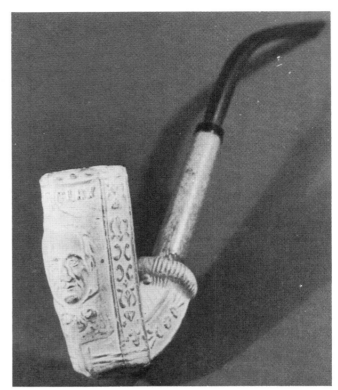

Henry Clay's bid for the presidency in 1844 as the Whig party candidate against James K. Polk produced this interesting old clay pipe. It carries the identification "Henry Clay" and shows his embossed features. One side of the stem has the wording, "Warranted to color." A surprising number of these old pipes have survived. The bowl is 2½" high. **$90**

Henry Clay looks youthful on this interesting leather cigar-holder made as a campaign item in 1844. The holder is pictured along with the insert. Clay is identified as "The American Statesman." A scarce artifact, it measures 5½" long × 3" wide. **$750**

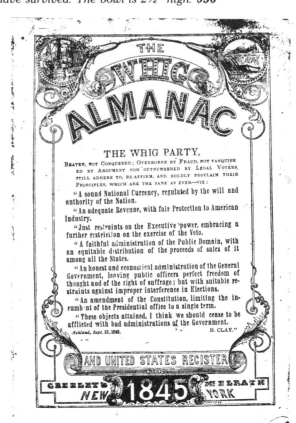

In 1845, after Whig candidate Henry Clay had long gone down to defeat at the hands of the Democratic Party's James K. Polk, this Whig Party Almanac had all the reasons why it happened—strictly from a Whig point of view. The cover notes that the Whigs were "beaten, not conquered; overborne by fraud, not vanquished by argument nor outnumbered by legal voters. . . ." The Almanac proudly bears the names of "Greeley & McElrath" and quotes Clay as advocating a constitutional amendment which would limit a president to "a single term" in office. In addition to politics, such almanacs also were filled with many interesting facts. **$10**

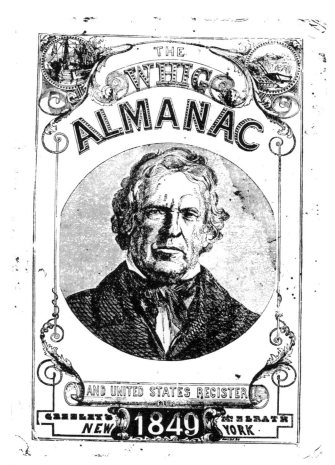

This General Zachary Taylor flask was made by the Dyottville Glass Works, Philadelphia in 1848 for Taylor's presidential campaign. The aquamarine flask carries Taylor's embossed image, showing five buttons on his coat, and it emphasizes the courageous slogan, "Gen. Taylor Never Surrenders." The other side pictures George Washington, "The Father of His Country." Although not easily found, Taylor flasks come in 28 variations; height, 7¼". **$140**

The Whig Party interpretation of the election of 1848 can be found along with many other details in this Whig Almanac and "United States Register" of 1849. A flattering sketch of President-elect Zachary Taylor adorns the cover. Interesting reading. **$22**

Two campaign items from Zachary Taylor's successful bid for the presidency in 1848 are shown here. At the left is a "Rough & Ready" clothing button. At the right is a Taylor medalet, produced in 1847 to extol Taylor's credentials as a military leader. Clothing button **$38**; Medalet **$30**

Millard Fillmore
1850–1853

Millard Fillmore appears on this early presidential paperweight, made by the New England Glass Company of East Cambridge, Massachusetts. It was probably produced in late 1850, since Fillmore was in office only from the time of Zachary Taylor's death until 1852. Moreover, the inscription surrounding his frosted intaglio image identifies him as "Millard Fillmore, President of the United States" and carries the "1850" date beneath his portrait. Hexagonal in shape, the Fillmore weight was made in limited quantity and is considered rare. It has beveled edges, is 3½" wide and nearly 1" high. Similar weights exist for Henry Clay and Daniel Webster. **$350**

A Millard Fillmore ribbon from 1856, when he ran with Andrew Donelson on the Know-Nothing ticket, is pictured here. **$500**

Franklin Pierce
1853–1857

"Gen. Frank Pierce, the Stateman Soldier," is the presidential candidate shown on this medalet from the campaign of 1852. Pierce was from New Hampshire while his running mate, William R. King, was from Alabama. **$35** (in good condition)

Made while he was in office, this battered field mirror with pewter case pictures "General Franklin Pierce, President of the United States." Highly valued by presidential collectors, it is extremely hard to find. A similar mirror also was made for Zachary Taylor. **$350**

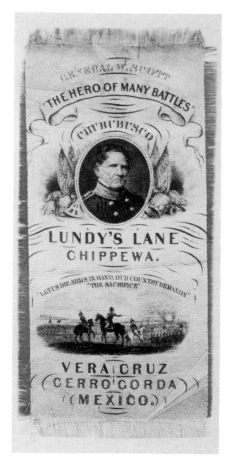

A rare jugate ribbon from the 1852 campaign is shown here. It pictures Franklin Pierce and William R. King, the successful Democratic Party candidates. Few collectors are able to display such a prize in their collection. The ribbon is 6½" long × 2½" wide. **$2,300**

This rare ribbon, showing General Winfield Scott as "The Hero of many Battles," was used to help promote him for the presidency in 1852. Above the battle scene on the lower half of the early campaign memento is the grim wording, "Let us die arms in hand, our country demands the sacrifice." **$400**

Crusty-looking Winfield Scott is shown on this great old lithograph published by A. Winch, 320 Chestnut Street, Philadelphia. The Whigs preferred Scott as their candidate in 1852 rather than the incumbent president, Millard Fillmore. Scott lost the election to Pierce by around 215,000 votes. The framed lithograph measures 17½" × 13½". **$125**

James Buchanan
1857–1861

Described as the "Birthplace of the Republican Party," a little schoolhouse in Ripon, Wisconsin, is pictured on these two pieces of souvenir china. The GOP was founded in 1854 and made John Fremont its first candidate for the White House. Their second candidate—Abraham Lincoln—was elected in 1860. The vase is 5" tall; the creamer measures 3¼". Each **$30**

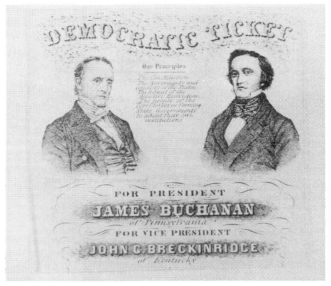

The Buchanan-Breckinridge democratic ticket is pictured on this paper ballot, along with a listing of "Our Principles"— which included a pledge to repeal the "Missouri Restriction." Unusual graphics make this an interesting collectible. **$50**

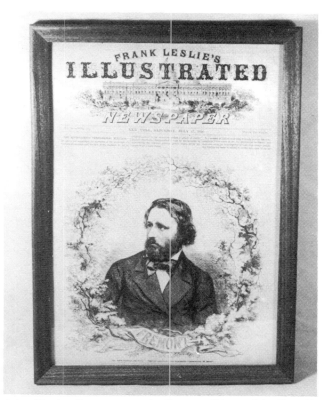

John Charles Fremont was the first candidate of the Republican Party in the presidential election of 1856. An explorer, army officer, and politician, Fremont made an attractive candidate but lost to Buchanan by about 500,000 votes. He is shown here in a framed cover of Frank Leslie's Illustrated, dated July 12, 1856. Fremont's likeness is identified as having been "Ambrotyped by Brady." **$30**

A campaign ribbon picturing James Buchanan for the election of 1856 not only lists the name of his running mate, John C. Breckinridge, but also adds a touch of humor with the words, "We Po'ked 'em in '44, We Pierced 'em in '52, And we'll 'Buck 'em in '56." Length, 7". **$285**

When John C. Fremont emerged as the presidential candidate of the newly formed Republican Party in 1856, this colored Kellogg print was one of the items used to make him more familiar to voters. A native of Georgia, Fremont gained his fame as an explorer, soldier, and politician. Though inclined to be somewhat headstrong, Fremont had the respect of his countrymen but lost the election to Buchanan by around 500,000 votes. The framed print is 17" × 14¼". **$135**

Losers in the presidential race in 1856 were John C. Fremont and Millard Fillmore, the latter running as the candidate of the American party, the "Know Nothings." The Fremont ribbon is 5" long, and the Fillmore ribbon measures 7¼". Fremont **$90**; Fillmore **$175**

Envelopes picturing the candidates were a popular campaign device during the late 1850s and the 1860s. This one, showing James Buchanan, makes the critical comment, "Look at what our country has been brought to under your Administration!" Such envelopes were used for both positive and negative partisan objecives. The envelope measures 5⅛" × 2⅞". **$25**

The first candidate of the new Republican Party, John C. Fremont, is shown on the medalet at the left which advocated a slogan of "Free Soil, Free Speech" in the 1856 election. The winner of that election, James Buchanan, is pictured on the medalet at the right. The slogan on the Buchanan medalet is "No Sectionalism." These are excellent and inexpensive presidential souvenirs from a momentous time in our nation's history. Fremont **$25**; Buchanan **$30**

Abraham Lincoln
1861–1865

"Lincoln at Home" is the name given to this Currier & Ives lithograph produced in 1867. It shows Mrs. Lincoln, Robert Lincoln, Tad, and the President. Still in the original 14" × 17" frame. **$125**

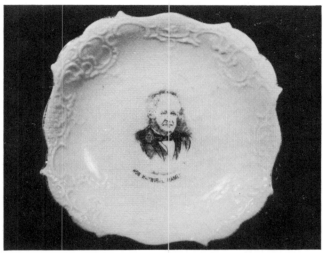

The Honorable Hannibal Hamlin is shown on this transfer souvenir china plate made in Germany for the Adams and Strickland firm of Bangor, Maine. The plate probably dates from before the turn of the century. Hamlin served as Lincoln's vice president during his first term. $85

Mathew Brady portrait-ribbons were made for candidates in the 1860 election, and this beauty, complete with facsimile signature, features the inspiring likeness of Abraham Lincoln. Others found on the Brady single-picture ribbons include John Breckinridge, Stephen Douglas, and John Bell. The Lincoln ribbon is 6½" long × 2½" wide. Scarce. $700

The dramatic setting for Abraham Lincoln's Gettysburg address is pictured on these two items made by the Homer Laughlin China Company for the firm's Historical America china set. Lincoln, shown talking to the crowd, is pictured in red on both sides of the gravy boat, which measures 8½" long × 3⅜" high. The serving bowl, which also has a red floral border, is 9½" × 7". Gravy boat $65; Serving bowl $45

It's only a facsimile, but this framed combination of a beardless Lincoln and an excellent copy of the Gettysburg Address holds the interest of presidential collectors. Lincoln's pioneer features and his handwriting seem to blend to emphasize the document's historic meaning. The frame is 25 × 9½". **$50**

Attractively framed and double matted, this autograph and striking picture of Stephen Douglas, who ran against Abraham Lincoln in the 1860 presidential election, has great appeal for those who enjoy the history of our nation's chief executives. The inked Douglas signature is clear and is recorded as "S. A. Douglas, Chicago, Ill." The frame is 13" × 17½". **$175**

Eagle torches were seen in political rallies as early as the 1840s and were still being used in nighttime marches at the time of Lincoln. Figural torches of this type captured the early excitement and patriotism of campaign supporters and are found more often in museums than in private collections. The torch is 10" high and 8¾" wide. **$750**

Collectors seeking a souvenir from the era of Lincoln would do well to look into the medalets produced for his campaigns. The one shown here was circulated in 1860, offering a side view of "Hon. Abraham Lincoln." The reverse of that same medalet is shown on the right, picturing Lincoln as "The Rail Splitter of the West." **$40** (in good condition)

Stephen A. Douglas, defeated by Abraham Lincoln in the 1860 presidential race, is remembered by this unusual handleless cup that shows his birthplace in Brandon, Vermont. An extremely delicate ceramic souvenir, the cup was made for the Charles H. Ross retail outlet in Brandon. It stands 2¼" high. **$85**

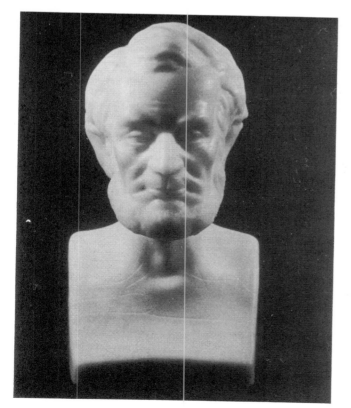

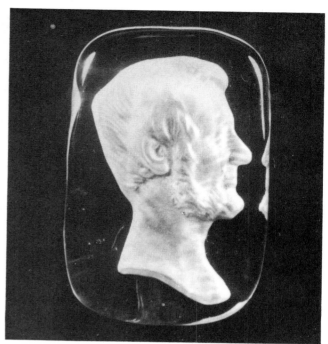

Abraham Lincoln collectors always have admired this heavy rectangular weight with the intaglio likeness of the great Civil War president. Good clear glass allows the frosted finish on Lincoln's features to be viewed from many angles. It's believed to have been made sometime between the 1876 Centennial and 1900, and it is 4⅜" long × 3" wide. **$125**

Mary Todd Lincoln, a somewhat tragic figure in American history, is pictured in color on this plate, one in a series believed made around 1909, during Lincoln's Centennial. Probably a giveaway, it's an attractive addition to any presidential collection. The back is marked "Imperial China" and "a remembrance from Zander-Pfeffer Co." It is 6" square. **$20**

Abraham Lincoln is honored in this expertly sculptured, acid-finish milk-white glass bust designed by P. J. Jacobus for Gillinder & Sons of Philadelphia at the time of the 1876 Centennial. The 6¼" bust has a hollow base, while others are solid and bear Centennial markings. It is also found in clear glass with an acid finish. At the time of the Centennial, the bust wholesaled for 75 cents each. Because of the fine workmanship and Lincoln's place in history, they now are highly prized by collectors. **$450**

This rather unusual Lincoln plate was made for a gathering of the Lincoln Park Chapter No. 177, Royal Arch Masons, in Chicago on February 12, 1910. Decorated in color with Lincoln's image and his birthplace, it features a letter President Lincoln wrote to Mrs. Bixby in Boston in 1864. Mrs. Bixby lost five sons in the Civil War. Lincoln's letter to her has been called an example of the "purest English" ever written. A fine collectible plate. Diameter, 8½". **$40**

A rare paper campaign lantern from 1864 when George Mc-Clellan, pictured on the lantern, opposed Abraham Lincoln. It is remarkable that such a delicate presidential artifact could survive, thus adding to its rarity. In addition to the obvious printing on the lantern, the other sides called for "Equity and Justice" and "Trial by Jury," 8" high × 8½" wide. **$450**

A smiling Lincoln is featured in this round paperweight made 11 years after his death by the Gillinder & Sons glass firm on the grounds of the 1876 Centennial in Philadelphia. The sides, the upper edge, and the intaglio impression of the Great Emancipator are acid-treated, or as many say, "frosted." It's a fine glass souvenir of a great president. The diameter is 3"; the height, 1". **$175**

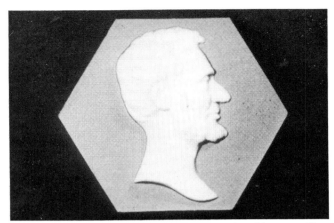

The bas-relief likeness of Lincoln appears in white on a blue tile made by the Allen Tiling Company of Chicago. It is 3" high × 3⅜" wide. **$25**

Some confusion exists regarding this full-color portrait plate of Abraham Lincoln. Actually, it is believed to date to around 1909, the time of the Lincoln Centennial, with one attribution listing it as a giveaway by the Teeds China Emporium. The reverse side shows an image believed to be the Liberty Bell, topped by the head of an eagle. Inside the bell is the marking, "The Colonial Co." It's a fine presidential memento; diameter, 8¼". **$50**

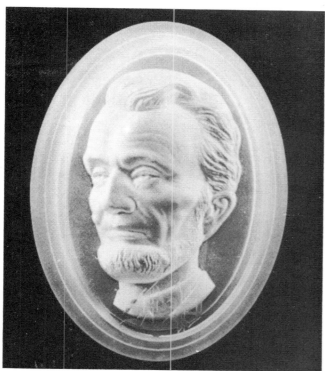

Lincoln's image is deeply impressed in the base of this oval paperweight made by Gillinder & Sons of Philadelphia; it sold at the time of the nation's Centennial celebration in 1876. The bottom and sides were treated with acid, with the top polished so as to emphasize Lincoln's features. The paperweight is 5½" long × 4" wide. It's an excellent piece of historical glass. **$225**

The advanced collector often assembles his collection in frames for easy viewing and display. This outstanding exhibit showing medals, tokens, ferrotypes, and ribbons is from the campaign of 1860 when Abraham Lincoln was elected. Such a collection is not only impressive because of its historic beauty, but is worth thousands of dollars.

After the assassination of Abraham Lincoln, a pattern glass was produced that is now known as "Lincoln Drape." This is a goblet showing the Lincoln Drape with tassel. Goblets were also made without the tassel. Glass historians have attributed this pattern to Sandwich, Massachusetts, with the possibility that it was made elsewhere also. It features good-quality lead glass and was first produced around 1866. Height, 6". **$95**

The type of derringer used by John Wilkes Booth to shoot Abraham Lincoln is pictured on the side of this little ceramic cup. The background scene shows Booth leaping onto the stage of the Ford Theater after the assassination. The cup is 3" high. **$25**

Abraham Lincoln was in office and looking weary from the stress of the Civil War when this ceramic mug bearing his likeness was manufactured. It is labeled "President Abraham Lincoln." The same transfer image of Lincoln can be found on an ABC plate. In reasonably good condition, these are scarce relics of a great president. The mug is 3¼" high. **$500**

Andrew Johnson
1865–1869

Impeachment tickets for the trial of President Andrew Johnson today have become collectible. The trial began in March of 1868 and ended on May 16 that year with Johnson's acquital. After his term as president, Johnson twice was an unsuccessful candidate for Congress but was elected to the United States Senate in 1874. He served in the Senate until his death on July 31, 1875. **$110**

Two stages in the life of Andrew Johnson are shown on the front page of this October 14, 1865 edition of Harper's Weekly. Americans were still trying to adjust to the idea of Johnson being in the White House, and the national press was providing background information so the public could get to know more about him. The pictures here show a scene from Johnson's past, his old tailor shop in Greenville, Tennessee, and a scene from the moment where he was said to be "pardoning rebels at the White House." Old issues of early newspapers are filled with items of historic interest and are worth collecting. **$5** (average issue)

Few mementos can be found from the presidency of Andrew Johnson. This 1¼" numismatic issue, however, is one of the exceptions, having been made while Johnson was in the White House. Above his profiled image is his name while below he is identified as "President U.S." **$75**

Ulysses S. Grant
1869–1877

Ulysses S. Grant, looking trim and handsome in his general's uniform, is shown here in the form of a hard-paste Parian bust that perhaps served as a campaign item. Careful attention has been paid to Grant's hair and features in this excellent presidential artifact. The bust stands 7" high and carries the identification "U. S. Grant" on the base. **$100**

Ulysses S. Grant's scandal-plagued administration prompted the creation of this "Tammany Bank," patented in 1873. You put a coin in the upright hand of the Tammany politician, and he quickly dumps in into his pocket. It should be noted, too, that a larger coin, such as a quarter, gets into the pocket faster than a penny. The bank is 5¾" high. **$165**

Ulysses S. Grant's intaglio image appears on the bottom of this glass tumbler along with his campaign slogan, "Let Us Have Peace." The tumbler stands 3½" high and is a worthy addition for collectors who like to find presidential memorabilia in glass. **$45**

Beautifully made, this heavy metal match-holder shows a handsome likeness of Ulysses S. Grant and served as a campaign item in 1872 when he won reelection by defeating Horace Greeley. Grant's image is surrounded by stars, American flags, cannon barrels and cannon balls. Beneath Grant's bow tie is the grated area used for scratching matches and, as might be assumed, it shows the wear of many years. The excellent design, scrollwork and extraordinary detail make this a first-rate collectible from Grant's second campaign. **$200**

"Let Us Have Peace" was the slogan for the Ulysses S. Grant-Schuyler Colfax team in the 1868 election. This paper ballot, which also pictures two handicapped veterans from the Civil War, lists other candidates in a hard-to-read, but imaginative manner. 7¾" × 4". **$40**

A cane that honors the memory of Grant makes an appropriate addition to any collection of presidential mementos. This one shows the old Civil War hero wearing a somewhat troubled expression, and it bears some of the scars of long usage. The metal cane head is 2⅝" high. **$110**

Excellent design makes this Ulysses S. Grant ceramic trinket box a fine piece of presidential Americana. It is believed to date from around 1868, when Grant was at his peak as a national war hero and the republican candidate for the presidency. The likeness of Grant is unusually good, and the base features the American eagle and shield. It stands close to 5½" high. **$200**

Showing the wear of years, the colorful ribbon and two shell badges nevertheless are valued items among political collectors. The red, white, blue, and black ribbon is 4½" long × 1⅛" wide. The jugate ferrotype, picturing Grant and his running mate in the 1868 campaign, Schuyler Colfax, shows the kind of flaking that cuts into the value of such a fine old campaign item. Embossed on the back is "Patent Applied For." The lower cardboard Grant also has flaws, but still shows a formidable candidate at a time when he was the hero of the nation. The round Grant item is a litle larger than a quarter. All are priced "as is." Ribbon **$80**; Jugate **$165**; Round cardboard **$95**

Wearing his Civil War uniform, Ulysses S. Grant is honored in this modern iron bank. While Grant had his problems as president, his stature as a military leader has remained strong in American history. Although it isn't old, the Grant bank merits a place in a presidential collection. Height, 5½". **$25**

Medalets turned out for the 1868 and 1872 elections are shown here, with the one on the left featuring "General U. S. Grant" as the 1868 republican candidate. The jugate in the center shows democrat Horatio Seymour and his running mate, Francis Blair. On the right is a medalet for Horace Greeley, who ran against Grant and lost in the 1872 presidential election. Grant **$25**; Seymour-Blair **$35**; Greeley **$30**

Ferrotypes from the 1872 campaign in which Ulysses S. Grant defeated Horace Greeley are shown in this lineup. At left is a jugate showing Grant and his running mate, Henry Wilson. Grant appears alone in the oval tintype in the center. At right is Greeley along with his vice presidential candidate, Benjamin Brown. All of these are highly desirable items.
Grant-Wilson **$900**; Grant **$185**; Greeley-Brown **$1,000**

They called him the "Pride of America" and the "People's Choice" in this ribbon turned out for Ulysses S. Grant. An interesting design, it measures 7¾" long. **$150**

The pictures of 18 presidents up to and including Ulysses S. Grant appear on this attractively designed engraving of the Dwight Company, made by the American Bank Note Company of New York. The border also honors 38 states. Turned out at the time of the Centennial, the engraving carries the 1776–1876 dates. It measures 9½" × 8½". **$75**

Marketed as a memorial to Ulysses S. Grant, this good-looking glass bread tray was made by Bryce, Higbee & Company, Pittsburgh, in 1885. The intaglio image of Grant, wearing his Civil War uniform, is centered amid a patterned design background. The plate is inscribed "The Patriot and Soldier," is still available, and is reasonably priced. The plate measures 9½" square, with the raised sides 1½" high. **$35**

Produced in several colors and in clear glass, the "Let Us Have Peace" plate is a memorial to Ulysses S. Grant and was manufactured shortly after he died in 1885. The center portrait pictures Grant in his general's uniform, and the wording gives the date of his birth and death. The border decoration features overlapping maple leaves. The plates are believed to have been made by more than one company. Diameter, 10⅜". Color $60; Clear $45

Ulysses S. Grant's home in Galena, Illinois, is shown on this souvenir china sugar holder. The house and surrounding trees are in good color. The piece was made in Dresden and was distributed in the United States by Wheelock & Company. This and other souvenir items were sold from the Old Grant Leather Store in Galena. Height, 3½". $30

Rutherford B. Hayes
1877–1881

Jugate ribbons made for the election of 1876 not only show the candidates but also tell what states they're from. The Hayes-Wheeler duo won in a much-disputed vote over the Tilden-Hendricks team. With Tilden having received a majority of the popular votes, the outcome was decided by an electoral commission—which raised new problems of partisanship before the matter was settled in favor of Hayes. It wasn't until March 2, 1877 that the public knew who would be inaugurated president on March 5, 1877. The ribbons are 4¼" long × 2¼" wide. Hayes-Wheeler $135; Tilden-Hendricks $145

The bas-relief features of Rutherford Hayes are pictured on this bronze presidential medal. The base of the bust carries the name "Morgan," and the reverse side shows the March 5, 1877, the date on which Hayes was inaugurated. A well-designed medal, it's diameter is 3". $50

Rare and unusual is this little jugate tin collar-box made to celebrate the 1877 inauguration of President Rutherford Hayes and his vice president, William Wheeler. Not only does it carry the pictures of "Our President and Vice President" along with the date, but it also shows a little 1870s girl standing on a ladder perched against a cherry tree. In the girl's hand, as she picks cherries, is this same kind of tin, thereby showing its practical value for children. The wording on the side says, "Cherry Ripe, Cleveland Collar Co." A charming presidential memento. The oval tin is 4¾" long and 3" deep. **$190**

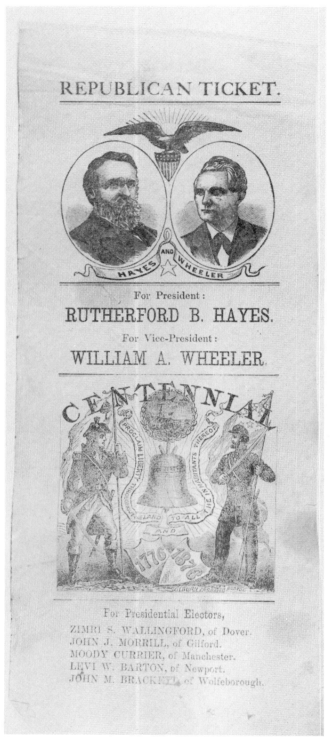

Both the presidential and Centennial themes are featured on this republican ballot turned out on behalf of republican candidates Rutherford Hayes and William Wheeler. **$50**

Rutherford B. Hayes is showcased in a little cigar-band dish of the kind that was common earlier this century. The picture is in rich color. Daniel Webster is shown on one of the cigar bands fanning out from the center. Diameter, 5". **$20**

Voters supported their candidates by wearing brass shells and other decorative portrait framings for the election of 1876, when Rutherford Hayes and Samuel Tilden were the opponents. Shown in this series are, left to right, Hayes and William Wheeler, Hayes, Tilden and Thomas Hendricks, and Tilden. *Hayes-Wheeler $250; Hayes $160; Tilden-Hendricks $275; Tilden $150*

The Hayes-Wheeler team sought the support of "The Boys in Blue" with this 1876 campaign ribbon. Uncluttered and attractive in its design, the ribbon is 5¼" long. *$140*

Backers of Tilden and Hendricks wore this ribbon proudly during the controversial election of 1876. Brightly decorated with the American eagle, stars, stripes, and the jugate likeness of the democratic candidates, this 4½" ribbon makes a fine campaign souvenir. *$175*

One of the more interesting campaign medalets is this one from our country's Centennial year in 1876. The face of the medalet shows Rutherford B. Hayes "For president of the United States." The reverse pictures the vice presidential candidate, William A. Wheeler. Both sides of the item also say "Centennial 1876 America." *$48* (good condition)

This miniature Liberty Bell mug was made by the Adams Glass Company of Pittsburgh during the presidential election year of 1876, when the nation also celebrated its centennial. Faintly embossed on the sides of the bell—and almost impossible to see, even when you hold the mug in your hands—are the names "Hayes" and "Wheeler;" it's also dated "1776–1876." Height, 2". Scarce. *$90*

James A. Garfield
1881

James A. Garfield, our second president to be assassinated, is remembered by this Bennington-type pitcher. His embossed image is surrounded by an ornate leafy border, with decorative trim also around the top, bottom, and on the handle. Probably manufactured in 1881 as a memorial piece. Not easily found, the pitcher stands 7½" high. **$300**

The facsimile signature of James A. Garfield identifies the presidential candidate on this ironstone plate made for the 1880 election. The transfer image of Garfield is dark and clear. A gold border decorates the rim. Diameter, 8". **$55**

Winfield S. Hancock was the democratic candidate who opposed James A. Garfield in the 1880 presidential campaign. It was a close race, and Hancock, a general who distinguished himself during the Civil War, was narrowly defeated. The ironstone plate showing his likeness was made for the campaign. It has a diameter of 7¾". **$50**

Three medalets from the 1880 election are pictured here, with democrats Winfield Hancock and his vice presidential partner, William English, shown on the left. The center jugate pictures James Garfield and his running mate, Chester Arthur, who became president when Garfield was assassinated by Charles Guiteau. The medalet on the right is the one most commonly found and lists his inauguration date on the back. Hancock-English **$28**; Garfield-Arthur **$30**; Garfield **$20**

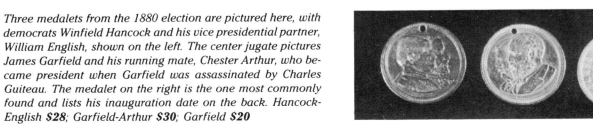

The Garfield-Arthur glass campaign mug pictured here is an outstanding example of presidential Americana. Just 2⅛" high, it shows James Garfield on one side and, on the other side, a fine likeness of a politically symbolic raccoon that appears to be thumbing its nose at the opposition. The handle is embossed on one side with the name "Garfield," and misspelled on the other side is the name of his running mate, "Arthurs." At the top of the handle is the date 1880. The maker is identified on the base as "Adams & Co. Glass Mfgrs." of Pittsburgh. *$175*

Collar boxes were popular back in 1880, when James Garfield ran for president. This one was made with his finely executed bas-relief likeness on the cover. The wooden boxes are 4¼" square and 3" deep. The bottom of this one also bears the license stamp of "The Standard Collar Company," originally licensed under a patent in October of 1872. Garfield's vice presidential mate, Chester Arthur, is shown on a companion box. *$135*

Made for his campaign against Winfield S. Hancock in 1880, this paperweight showing the image of James A. Garfield is not easily found. It's clear glass, 3¼" in diameter, and ¾" thick; and it has Garfield's intaglio features highlighted with an acid finish. A matching weight was made for Hancock. This is an excellent campaign souvenir from one of our assassinated presidents. *$200*

Two jugate bandannas made for the campaign of 1880 manage to combine appropriate flag-waving with the desired political message. The top bandanna shows James Garfield and his running mate, Chester Arthur. The more ornate textile at the bottom pictures Winfield S. Hancock and his vice presidential candidate, William H. English. Both are fine campaign items. *Garfield-Arthur $190; Hancock-English $225*

Possibly a campaign item, this nicely decorated glass plate features a fine intaglio image of James A. Garfield and a border that has 13 stars, two flags, and a shield. The Garfield likeness is acid-etched. The plate appears to have been made by the Crystal Glass Company of Bridgeport, Ohio. Still available, the plates are reasonably priced for their age and quality. Diameter, 6". **$45**

This Garfield piece has been called at various times a cup plate or an ashtray, but it's the author's view that it more likely is a little pin tray. Made of thick, sturdy glass, the 3" tray has an excellent intaglio image of Garfield and makes a fine presidential glass collectible. Probably a campaign item, the Crystal Glass Company of Bridgeport, Ohio is believed to be the manufacturer. Hard to find. **$60**

Called the martyr's mug, the bas-relief images of both Abraham Lincoln and James Garfield appear on the sides of this historic glass memento. The dates of their births and assassinations also are shown, and the wreathlike handle is decorated with stars. Made after the death of Garfield by the Adams Glass Company of Pittsburgh. Height, 2½". In the author's view, this unusual piece has remained a bargain. **$70**

A plaster bust, 12" high, was made as a memorial to James Garfield after his assassination. His name is impressed into the back. Scrawled in pencil on the back by some long-ago owner is September 19, 1881, the date of Garfield's death, along with the mournful comment "A noble hero." Personal notes of this kind on old presidential collectibles sometimes provide added historic perspective. **$45**

After Garfield's death, the Adams Glass Company of Pittsburgh changed the mold of its Garfield-Arthur campaign mug to make it a memorial item. The raccoon was removed from one side and was replaced by birth and death dates surrounded by a mourning drape. Garfield's image remains on the other side, but the names of Garfield and Arthur have been removed from the handle. Overlooked, however, was the fact that the top of the handle still carried the "1880" campaign mug date—even though the memorial mug was made for the market after Garfield's death in 1881. This mug is a fine presidential memento. Height, 2⅛". **$100**

Garfield's portrait surrounded by a wreath in the base of this tumbler presumably makes it a memorial item turned out after his assassination in 1881. Height, 3½". **$50**

"God reigns and the government at Washington still lives" says some of the emotional wording on this framed "memento of 1881." It was produced to honor "the departed soul of our martyr president," James Garfield. It also carries a copyright from James Meyer, Jr. dating to 1881. Framed, the memento is 14" × 11½". **$45**

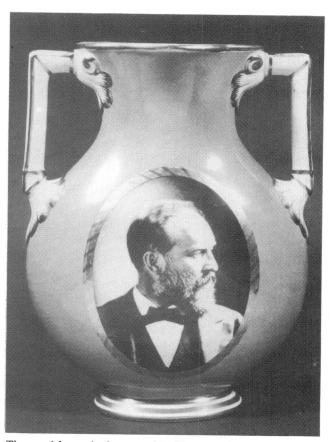

The oval-framed photographic likeness of President James Garfield is clearly pictured on this rare pink luster vase. It's the only one that the author has ever seen. The owner of the vase, a political collector of many years, says he is aware of just one other vase similar to it. Gracefully designed, it's trimmed in gold and stands 9" high. **$1,275**

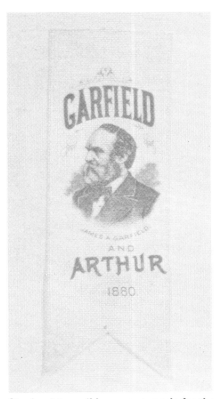

Single-picture ribbons were made for the candidates in both major parties for the 1880 campaign. This one pictures the winner, Garfield. **$125**

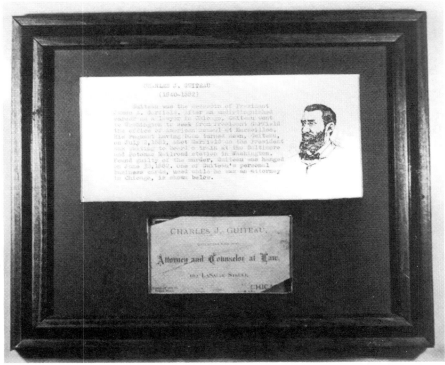

This framed personal business card is from Charles J. Guiteau, the man who was hanged for assassinating President Garfield. The card was used by Guiteau when he was a lawyer in Chicago. Angry when his request for a diplomatic post was turned down, Guiteau shot President Garfield at a railroad station in Washington on July 2, 1881. It's an unusual souvenir of one of our murdered presidents. Guiteau's card, boasting of "seven years' practice" and promising "law business promptly attended to," measures 4" × 2¼". **$100**

James Garfield's death immediately linked him with the assassinated Lincoln. This somber display was featured on a stereo card made by the Littleton View Company of Littleton, New Hampshire. Size: 7" × 3½". **$6**

A large commemorative glass plate was made in the Garfield Drape pattern after the death of President Garfield. The fallen president is framed by the words "We Mourn Our Nation's Loss," which are set against a stippled background. The dates that Garfield was born, shot, and died are on the plate, along with stars and floral decorations. It's attributed to the Adams Glass Company, Pittsburgh. Diameter, 11⅜". **$60**

This memorial plate honors the memory of President James Garfield, who died September 19, 1881 after having been shot on July 2, 1881 by Charles Guiteau, who had been seeking a government appointment. The plate has a stippled border, with Garfield's image surrounded by a laurel design and the single word "Memorial." Made by the Adams Glass Company, Pittsburgh. **$45**

Known by two names, the "In Remembrance" and "Three Presidents" tray, this heavy glass platter makes a worthy addition to any presidential collection. The central theme features the framed portraits of Washington, Lincoln, and Garfield. The tray was made after the assassination of Garfield and has a stippled laurel-wreath border. It's a good historical piece and is appropriate for anyone hunting for memorabilia of our presidents. Length, 12½". **$65**

One of the most attractive little ABC plates turned out by American glassmakers for political as well as practical purposes is this one made as a tribute to Garfield. Perhaps manufactured for his campaign, it shows the frosted intaglio likeness of Garfield surrounded by the alphabet. Children loved the plates, and so did their parents. It's believed to have been made by the Crystal Glass Company of Bridgeport, Ohio. Diameter, 6". **$55**

Clothing buttons from the 1880 campaign between James Garfield and Winfield Hancock make sturdy campaign souvenirs for the collector. These brass buttons urge support for "Garfield and Arthur" and "Hancock and English." Each measures ¾" in diameter. Each **$25**

Chester A. Arthur
1881–1885

He didn't know it when this plate was made, but Chester A. Arthur was destined to be president. The ironstone plate, with a diameter of 8", pictures him "For Vice President." An assassin's bullet put him into office for most of what would have been the term of James A. Garfield. The plate has black trim on the rim. **$60**

Chester A. Arthur left comparatively few collectibles, since he was not nominated by the republicans in 1884 after having served as president following the assassination of President James Garfield. This collar box was made for the 1880 campaign when he ran with Garfield. It is 4¾" square and 3" deep. **$140**

Grover Cleveland
1885–1889
1893–1897

Made for the 1884 campaign, this jugate glass tray pictures the democratic candidates Grover Cleveland and Thomas Hendricks. It is an example of the great designs of P. J. Jacobus, who freelanced his talents, but it's most closely identified with the Gillinder & Sons glassworks of Philadelphia. The names of the candidates appear on their images, which are frosted. The border of this handled tray is decorated with a stippled leaf design. The tray is 11½" wide × 8½" high. **$250**

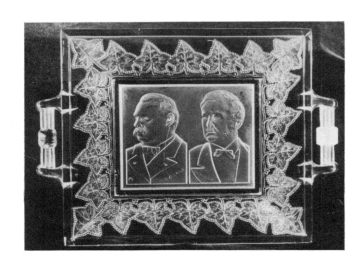

The 1884 campaign between Grover Cleveland and James G. Blaine may have been politically "dirty," but it nevertheless produced many first-rate collectibles. Included are these two well-made metal pins worn by those who supported the candidates. Each is 2¾" long. Each **$30**

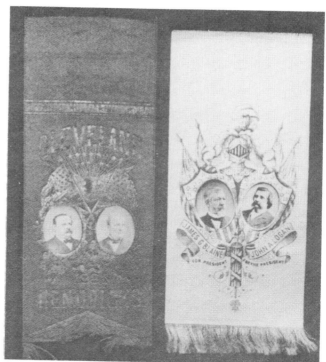

Jugate ribbons made for the 1884 election show Cleveland and Hendricks on the left and Blaine and Logan on the right. Collectors like to find similar items supporting the candidates of the major parties. Each **$100**

Something different in the way of presidential collectibles is this framed paper bookplate from a Civil War general, Edward S. Bragg. The brave little Iron Brigade hero, who also served in Congress, delivered a now-familiar epigram when he nominated Grover Cleveland at the 1884 convention and challenged Tammany in the process. "They love him, gentlemen," he declared, "and they respect him, not only for himself, but they love him most for the enemies he has made." Bragg himself received party votes for the presidential nomination in 1896. The bookplate is 3" × 4¼". **$25**

John A. Logan, who was defeated as the vice presidential candidate with James G. Blaine in 1884, is pictured on this unusual metal canteen. Logan, who also is credited as the founder of Memorial Day, was a leader in the Grand Army of the Republic. The canteen, which has an attached chain for carrying, perhaps was manufactured to help whip up political support among his old Civil War buddies. Above Logan's transfer picture is the slogan, "We drank from the same canteen." From spout to bottom, the canteen measures 5¼". Scarce. **$200**

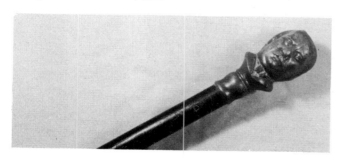

Well-worn from long use, this old campaign cane handle is made in the image of Grover Cleveland. The metal cane head is 3¼" high. **$110**

Rarely found is this large glass hat probably made for the election of 1888 when Cleveland lost to Benjamin Harrison. It is much larger than the smaller glass hats made for the 1892 election. The hat shows Cleveland in a frosted oval along with the wording "For President." The other side carries the message, "The same old hat." It is 4¼" high, and the brim has a diameter of 6¾". **$150**

Grover Cleveland was in the White House when this attractive majolica tray was made in his honor in Germany. Cleveland's photo is under the glaze along with the wording "Grover Cleveland, President of the United States." An unusual and scarce item, the tray is 9" × 6¼". **$160**

An ironstone plate with a worn gold border shows James G. Blaine at the time he ran for the presidency in 1884. It was a dirty campaign, and Blaine's loss was attributed in part to an anti-Catholic slur made by one of his backers. A good old campaign souvenir, the plate has a diameter of 8". **$45**

The four Classic Pattern portrait plates designed for the 1884 presidential campaign rank as historic glass artistry at its finest. This one pictures Grover Cleveland and is characterized, as are all the plates, by great emphasis on lifelike detail. The plates are hard to find and rank as the best ever produced in the political glass category. Diameter, 11½". **$235**

A companion plate to the one picturing James G. Blaine during his 1884 campaign for the presidency shows John A. Logan, who ran with Blaine as the candidate for vice president. Logan organized the GAR and served on the impeachment committee at the time that Andrew Johnson was president. The diameter of the plate measures 8". *$45*

Signed by P. J. Jacobus, the gifted moldmaker who fashioned the four Classic Pattern political plates, this plate features the likeness of Thomas Hendricks, the running mate of Cleveland in the 1884 campaign. The signature of Jacobus is found at the lower edge of Hendricks' right shoulder. The two other Classic plates that were made showed similar acid-finish portraits of James Blaine and John Logan. In all, the glassmaking quality is unexcelled. Diameter, 11½". *$240*

The metal rooster appears to be crowing atop this simple though attractive Cleveland and Hendricks ribbon made for the presidential campaign of 1884. In all, it is 8¾" long × 2½" wide. *$60*

Jugate medalets from the 1884 campaign featured democrats Grover Cleveland and Thomas Hendricks and republican candidates James Blaine and John Logan. Cleveland-Hendricks *$20*; Blaine-Logan *$20*

There were many china plates circulated in 1884 to help the election chances of James G. Blaine, and this navy blue portrait campaign item was one of them. The border also is trimmed in blue. Diameter, 8". **$45**

Thomas Hendricks, who ran with Cleveland in 1884, was installed as vice president in March 1885, but he died in November that same year. This plate was made as one of a pair for the democratic candidates; it is Royal Ironstone China, made by Johnson Brothers, England. Diameter, 8½". **$45**

Made by Johnson Brothers, England, this Cleveland plate was produced as one of a campaign set for the election of 1884. It's made of good-quality ironstone. The other plate in the set pictures Cleveland's vice presidential candidate, Thomas Hendricks. Diameter, 8½". **$50**

Grover Cleveland's portrait is pressed into the bottom of this clear glass tumbler. It's probably a campaign item from 1884. Height, 3½". **$50**

The 1884 campaign of Grover Cleveland and Thomas Hendricks is remembered by this star-decorated old "C & H" belt buckle. Length, 3¼"; width, 2¼". **$30**

Well-defined facial features and darker hair make this Grover Cleveland plate a little different than some of the others. It was probably manufactured for the campaign of 1884. Diameter, 8". **$50**

Grover Cleveland's years as president are recalled in this excellently detailed plaster bust, made for use as a paperweight or to hang on a wall. Probably made during his first term in office from 1884–1888. Height, 6". **$25**

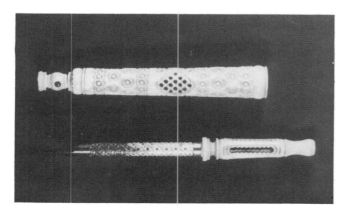

Made for the 1884 campaign, this 6" ironstone creamer shows a familiar portrait of Cleveland, with Hendricks, his running mate, on the other side. **$100**

Brooms and a rooster decorate this interesting 1888 campaign scarf made to promote "Our Candidates," Grover Cleveland and Allen Thurman. The scarf is 18½" square. **$185**

Even stanhopes played a role in popularizing our American presidents. This one also served as a pen. When not in use, the pen was inserted into the ivory holder, and the owner could enjoy the thrill of looking through that little hole near the end and seeing—lo and behold!—"President Cleveland." When closed, the pen is 5½" long. Little metal pig stanhopes also were used for less flattering political purposes. **$100**

This heavy ironstone compote is from the unsuccessful campaign of Grover Cleveland's attempt at a second term in 1888. Cleveland and his democratic vice presidential candidate, Allen Thurman, are pictured in reddish-brown transfer images inside the bowl. It is an unusual jugate piece of presidential campaign china. The bowl has a diameter of 8¾", and the compote stands 4¾" high. **$210**

Finding one of these delicate kerosene lamp chimneys from a presidential race poses a real challenge for the collector. This beauty shows Allen Thurman set against a flag-decorated frosted glass background, with a similar portrait of Cleveland on the other side. Thurman was Cleveland's vice presidential partner in the 1888 election. The chimney is 8" high. **$300**

A good transfer likeness of Grover Cleveland appears on this ironstone mug made by G.M. & Son of East Liverpool, Ohio. An unusual item, 5½" tall. **$95**

Grover Cleveland and Benjamin Harrison faced each other twice and split the spoils of victory. Harrison won over Cleveland in 1888; in 1892, Cleveland reversed that decision. Each is shown on a campaign ribbon that collectors find attractive. Each **$60**

Grover Cleveland and his 1892 vice presidential candidate Adlai Stevenson are pictured on opposite sides of this clever brass pillbox. The box is shaped like four stacked coins and bears the 1892 date along with the inscription, "My Stack on Cleveland." A similar pillbox was made for Benjamin Harrison and Whitelaw Reid. It's a good addition to any political collection. **$70**

Grover Cleveland had just taken office for his second nonconsecutive term as president when this metal bust was made for national distribution. It is made well and has an excellent likeness. Cleveland's name is on the front of the bust and an 1893 copyright date is on the back. It stands 8½" tall. **$60**

Encircled in the base of this unusual round paperweight is the picture of Grover Cleveland. The weight probably was made for Cleveland's 1892 bid for the presidency, when he defeated Benjamin Harrison. Diameter, 3". **$100**

In 1892, when Grover Cleveland was elected to a second nonconsecutive term in the White House, he ran with Adlai E. Stevenson, whose grandson would be a candidate for president 60 years later. This jugate ribbon, bright with color, is from the 1892 campaign. Length, 6¼". **$95**

Metal-framed cardboard portraits of the candidates were turned out for the 1884 election, along with brass clothing buttons. Cleveland is shown on the left, and Blaine is to the right. The top button urges support for Blaine-Logan and the other has the embossed names of Cleveland-Hendricks. *Cleveland $80; Blaine $65; Blaine-Logan $30; Cleveland-Hendricks $25*

The large medalet at left features Cleveland and the famous quotation, "a public office is a public trust." On the right, a jugate numismatic collectible shows the GOP nominees for the 1892 presidential race, Benjamin Harrison and Whitelaw Reid. Cleveland defeated Harrison's bid for reelection and thereby earned an unusual place in presidential history by winning his own, though nonconsecutive, second term. *Cleveland $35; Harrison $40*

Benjamin Harrison
1889–1893

A campaign egg for 1888 shows a gold-plated tin rooster crowing for Harrison and Morton. Made of wood, these eggs operated by way of an inner spring arrangement that made the rooster pop up with its political mesage. Many were given away by merchants as sales gimmicks in 1888, and few are found in perfect working order today. Yet they're excellent souvenirs of the old presidential campaign process. With the rooster crowing, this one measures 3½" high. *$225*

Made to look like Benjamin Harrison, this metal match holder was patented in time to be used in the campaign of 1888. The latch opens at the base, and there's a rough surface for match-scratching on the bottom. A fine presidential item, it stands 2¾" high. *$140*

Benjamin Harrison and Levi Morton are shown in this coveted jugate glass tray designed by P. J. Jacobus for the 1888 campaign. A similar tray also was made for Cleveland and Thurman. The same stippled leaf borders used on trays made for the 1884 campaign were used in 1888, although on the later trays there are no handles. The portraits of the candidates are frosted. The tray is 9½" wide, 8½" high. **$250**

This jugate campaign ribbon from 1888 shows Benjamin Harrison and Levi Morton, and it also makes a play on the Harrison heritage from the Log Cabin presidential campaign of 1840. It has fine color and is well illustrated. Length, 6¼". **$135**

Benjamin Harrison appears on this ironstone plate, probably made for his campaign in 1888 against Grover Cleveland. The transfer print shows the sketched image of Harrison, and the plate has gold trim on both the inner and the outer borders of the rim. Diameter, 8". **$50**

This glass campaign hat, made for Benjamin Harrison's second race against Grover Cleveland in 1892, plays upon the memories of his grandfather, President William H. Harrison. The 2¼" hat bears the slogans, "The Same Old Hat" and "He's All Right." They were made in clear and milk glass, and were manufactured by the United States Glass Company. **$85**

Benjamin Harrison is the presidential subject of this hard-to-find tile made by C. Pardee Works, Perth Amboy, New Jersey. Harrison's well-defined embossed likeness on the purplish-brown tile is enhanced by a heavy glaze. The tile is 6" × 6" and is sought after by political collectors. **$80**

Presidential campaign bookmarks were circulated for the 1888 election with the candidates pictured on celluloid. Their celluloid images were fastened to red, white, and blue ribbons, highlighted by frontal bows. Grover Cleveland is shown on the left, while Benjamin Harrison, who won the election, is on the right. The reverse of the Harrison souvenir says, "Manufactured by J. O. Hardesty, Anderson, Ind." They are each 4¾" long × 2" wide. Each **$38**

Log cabin mustard jars were manufactured by the United States Glass Company for Benjamin Harrison in his losing 1892 campaign against Grover Cleveland. The jars also had little "roof" tops that were easily broken, and thereafter most of them became toothpick or match holders. The Tecumseh name above the door was another reminder that Harrison's grandfather was President William H. Harrison. A symbolic campaign item, it's hard to find. **$125**

Sun-faded pictures of Benjamin Harrison and Levi Morton, plus a hand-printed slogan, "Harrison and Morton and Protection to American Industries" show this to be an old homemade jugate paperweight. Scrawled in well-worn pencil writing on the base is this personal message, "Nov. 2, 1888. Harrison will carry N. York by 40,000 and Ind. by 6,000, and he will take his seat and don't you forget it. G. E. Davis." That's what you call real political fervor. Size, 4" × 2⅝". **$90**

Campaign cups made for the presidential election of 1888 carried the embossed images of the candidates. This one features Benjamin Harrison on one side and the vice presidential candidate, Levi Morton, on the other. A matching cup was made for Grover Cleveland and Allen Thurman. The cups also are found in amber as well as clear glass. Scarce. Height, 3". **$85**

This seldom-seen trivet featuring the center image of Benjamin Harrison framed by a horseshoe may have been a campaign item in 1888. Ferrotypes with Harrison inside a brightly colored enameled horseshoe pin inscribed with the words "Luck" and "Victory" were made for the 1888 race. The Harrison trivet is 5" long. **$90**

In a familiar political rally chant, the crowd would shout, "What's the matter with Harrison?" And in a roar would come the reply, "He's all right!" That kind of noisy performance led to the design of this delightful and rare platter, made for Harrison's campaign against Grover Cleveland. The hobnail border, the lettering, and the centering of the candidate's portrait is like the "Reform" plate made for Cleveland. Harrison's image is frosted. It is the author's view that this plate, which has a diameter of 10", was made by Bryce, Higbee & Company of Pittsburgh. **$225**

Stars decorate this old campaign torch used to enliven political gatherings as voters whooped it up for their favorite candidate. There are many varieties of torches, and some collectors specialize in that category. Prices vary, with rarities justifiably expensive. **$65**

Voters were reminded of presidential candidate Benjamin Harrison when they drank from this attractive ironstone mug showing Harrison's photographic likeness. An excellent souvenir, items such as this are scarce. Height, 4¼". **$90**

Another well-made ribbon from the last quarter of the nineteenth century picturing Benjamin Harrison and Whitelaw Reid, this one was produced for the GOP losers in the 1892 presidential election. In bright red, white, and blue colors, the ribbon is 6¼" long. **$95**

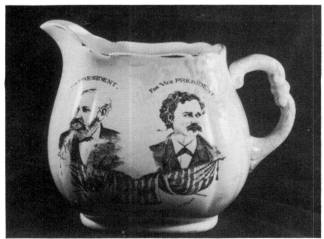

Benjamin Harrison, seeking reelection to a second term, had Whitelaw Reid as his running mate in the 1892 election. Both are shown on this Dresden china campaign pitcher, with their transfer images appearing on both sides. Collectors seek jugate items, so this scarce 6½" pitcher goes fast when it occasionally appears on the market. **$210**

"One good term deserves another" says the slogan above "the Harrison hat" pictured on the base of this domed 1892 campaign paperweight. It was made to promote a second term for Benjamin Harrison, with Whitelaw Reid as his vice presidential nominee. It's marked "Harrison & Reid" and carries the Latin inscription, "In hoc signo vinces," which translates to something like, "By this sign we shall win." (They lost.) Diameter, 3". **$85**

This inexpensive medalet for Benjamin Harrison is a heavily worn example from 1888. The reverse lists Harrison as "Republican candidate for President." **$15**

Sought after by historical glass collectors as well as those who pursue presidential Americana, this frosted glass statuette of Benjamin Harrison was probably made for his 1888 campaign. The statuette stands 5¾" high and, as this photo shows, is well designed. Of added interest is the fact that it was produced to fit atop a tall, black amethyst fluted pedestal bottle. Even without the base, which adds about $125 more to the price, the statuette is an impressive and scarce souvenir of Harrison's presidency. **$200**

Even dogs and cats got into the act when Grover Cleveland and Benjamin Harrison were presidential opponents. The hard-to-find milk-glass plate pictured here shows a dog and two cats above the slogan "He's all right." Generally, that slogan was applied to Harrison, who won the 1888 election but lost in 1892. Diameter, 6¼". **$90**

William McKinley
1897–1901

The designer of this 1896 campaign paperweight put his own name on it, lower center, along with the date. He called William McKinley "A winner" and mentioned the McKinley slogan of "Protection" and "Prosperity," while placing the words "Sound Money" above the head of vice presidential nominee Garret Hobart. The designer goofed, however, by misspelling McKinley as "McKinlly." An amusing memento, 4" long × 2½" wide. **$65**

Matching hatpins were made for William McKinley and his frail wife, Ida, for the campaign of 1896. The "Protection" slogan is on the McKinley hatpin, while the one showing Mrs. McKinley is brightly adorned with a colored ribbon. Each pin is 6" long. Each $30

It's hard to imagine an old-time political campaign without the vision of some voters being lured to the polls by a few swigs of whiskey. The label is a little worse for wear, but this old whiskey bottle survived from the 1896 campaign when William McKinley and his vice presidential partner, Garret Hobart, advocated the gold standard. The labels are in color. Poor condition of the label lowers the price on this one. Height, 6½". $35 (in condition shown)

A jugate plate made for the 1896 campaign shows photographic transfers of the winners, William McKinley and Garret Hobart. Marked on the back is "Semi-Vitreous" beneath a crown-topped trademark. Diameter, 9". $50

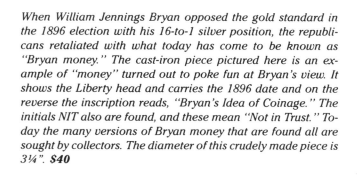

When William Jennings Bryan opposed the gold standard in the 1896 election with his 16-to-1 silver position, the republicans retaliated with what today has come to be known as "Bryan money." The cast-iron piece pictured here is an example of "money" turned out to poke fun at Bryan's view. It shows the Liberty head and carries the 1896 date and on the reverse the inscription reads, "Bryan's Idea of Coinage." The initials NIT also are found, and these mean "Not in Trust." Today the many versions of Bryan money that are found all are sought by collectors. The diameter of this crudely made piece is 3¼". $40

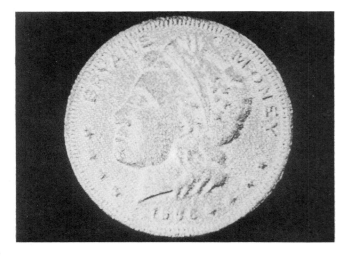

Bryan is shown in this fragile chimney for a kerosene lamp made for the campaign of 1896. The photographic image of Bryan is framed in an oval, with hand-painted flowers on each side. The top of the chimney is crimped and the decorated center area is frosted. Few of these delightful campaign reminders have survived. Height, 8½". **$300**

After his election in 1896, Americans wanted McKinley to "sweep clean" with a new broom. This little novelty broom, 5¼" long, was a means of expressing McKinley's political mission. Hard to find, even with the image of McKinley somewhat faded. **$65**

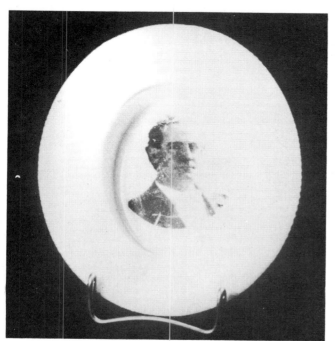

Straw hats were in vogue in 1896 when McKinley and Bryan became locked in the gold vs. silver campaign. The hatband on the little hat made for McKinley is gold, while the hatband on the one shown here is silver for Bryan. The inside of each hat pictured the candidate. Here we see Bryan. Made by McKee & Brothers of Pittsburgh as campaign pin-tray novelties. They are 1" deep and 4" long. **$95**

Among the paperweights turned out for President McKinley were these made in the form of seven-pointed stars, showing the president and his wife, Ida. The domed centers of the matching paperweights are surrounded by a beaded ring which some glass historians believe is designed to create an electric lightbulb effect in a era when such lights were still new. The paperweights are each 5" wide. President McKinley $65; Mrs. McKinley $40

An outstanding campaign piece, this little glass toothpick holder was manufactured to promote the candidacy of William Jennings Bryan and his vice presidential running mate, Arthur Sewall, in the gold standard vs. free coinage of silver race of 1896. Not only does the item have the symbolism of stacked silver coins as the "holder," but it also has the political rooster as a handle. In addition, embossed on the base, are the names "Bryan & Sewall" along with the slogan "16 to 1 Silver." Believed made by the United States Glass Company. Rare. $200

A rare cast-iron clock advocating the candidacy of William McKinley in the 1896 campaign features a dial made in the shape of a coin that reads, "Sound Money," and carries the date 1896. Topped by a bust of McKinley, the clock also is decorated with symbols of commerce in line with the McKinley slogan of "Protection-Prosperity." An exceptional item, 14½" high. $850

A jugate paperweight pictures the 1896 vice presidential candidate, Garret Hobart, on the left and presidential candidate William McKinley on the right. Usually the candidates are shown the other way around. An interesting campaign weight, 4" × 2½". $40

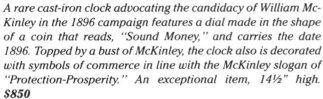

The full dinner pail was one of the symbols used by the political forces of William McKinley in the 1896 campaign against William Jennings Bryan. Cleverly made with a wire handle and a metal cup for a top, the pail is 4½" high from the spout to the base. It's a fine campaign artifact and is difficult to find. **$210**

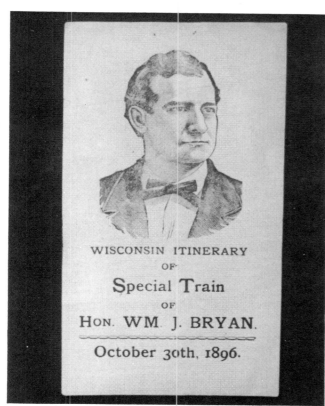

Whistle-stopping gained acceptance as an effective campaigning technique in 1896, when William Jennings Bryan spoke to audiences in many small communities. This illustrated paper schedule of his "Special Train" covered only one day, October 30, 1896, and on that day he stopped in 15 communities in Wisconsin. The itinerary noted that Bryan would "speak from the rear end of his car." Size, 5¾" × 3½". **$8**

Probably made for the 1896 campaign, this plate pictures a rather grim looking William McKinley along with his slogan, "Patriotism, Protection, Prosperity." The reverse side is marked "E.L.P. Co., Waco, China." Diameter, 9". **$40**

William Jennings Bryan's attempt to win the presidency on the issue of advocating the free coinage of silver is not overlooked in the decoration on this cane head from the 1896 campaign. Well-designed and interesting, the metal head is 3½" long. **$110**

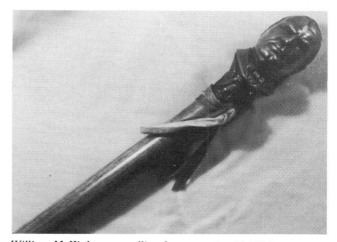

William McKinley was calling for protection in 1896, and that's the message on this impressive cane head used by his followers in the campaign against William Jennings Bryan. A fine presidential collectible. The head of the cane measures 3½". **$110**

This campaign tumbler portrays a steady-eyed William McKinley under the heading, "Our Next President," which was made for the campaign of 1896. Etched on the back of the 3½" blown tumbler in large letters is "Emma, 1896." At this stage in history, it seems rather nice to know that Emma's man won. **$65**

"Protection and Plenty" is the McKinley campaign slogan surrounding his image that is impressed in the bottom of this clear glass tumbler. Made for the 1896 campaign by McKee & Brothers of Pittsburgh. Height, 3¾". **$55**

Among the most attractive political glass pieces ever manufactured is this 9" Gothic border, milk-white ribbon plate picturing William McKinley in bas-relief. The likeness of McKinley appears in gold, and the ribbon decorating the border is gold to emphasize the 1896 gold vs. silver issue. Designed by David Baker, the plates were produced by the Canton Glass Company of Marion, Indiana. Because of their beauty, an impressive number of these plates have survived by being passed along in families. **$140**

A rare black amethyst glass ribbon plate with the bas-relief image of William Jennings Bryan made for the 1896 presidential campaign is a highly desirable political collectible. On some of the plates, Bryan's image may be found painted silver, just as the face of William McKinley on the milk-white Gothic border plates often is found painted gold. The ribbon in the border of the plate shown here is silver, an appropriate color for the campaign. Black amethyst plates showing either Bryan or McKinley are extremely hard to find and should be treasured. **$225**

Soap babies were made for the presidential campaign of 1896 between William McKinley and William Jennings Bryan. This was the gold vs. silver campaign, and babies were packaged in boxes that emphasized that political issue. Each baby was tagged with a little card telling why "My Papa will vote for . . ." (either McKinley or Bryan). Finding these soap babies in good condition, particularly without broken feet, is difficult. Each baby is 4¼" long, and the boxes are a main part of their value. Each $60

A tin horn was blown for "Patriotism, Protection, Prosperity" promised in the 1896 campaign of William McKinley, and it still blows with gusto. The campaign slogan is imprinted in the tin. A good souvenir of the excitement of past campaigns. Height, 4¼". $60

This heavy metal bust combines the look of antiquity with reasonably accurate facial detail, adding to its appeal as a presidential collectible. Probably made around the time of the 1896 campaign. The front of the base is marked "Wm McKinley," and on the reverse is "G. B. Haines, Chicago." Height, 7". $50

William McKinley looks out soberly from inside this thick paperweight, which probably was circulated for the campaign of 1896. Beneath the picture, in a facsimile of his own writing, is "Yours truly, Wm McKinley." Length 4", width 2½". $50

This McKinley plate, made in 7" and 9" sizes, was produced for the 1896 campaign between McKinley and Bryan. Made of sturdy glass, it carries the shielded image of McKinley, his "Protection and Plenty" slogan, and a starred border. Glass researcher and author William Heacock (in the Antique Trader, February 7, 1979) stated that the plates were advertised in an 1896 trade publication "prior to the elections." Still offered rather frequently on the market, the rope-edged plates are worthy of any collection of presidential memorabilia. **$45**

"Pennsylvania will head the column," says this domed paperweight, picturing William McKinley. The insert in the paperweight was made for the 1896 campaign. Diameter, 3". **$35**

Garret Hobart, the vice presidenial candidate with William McKinley in 1896, is shown on the reverse side of this highly prized 10" campaign pitcher that features McKinley's likeness on the other side. Hobart died on November 2, 1899, and the office was not filled until the election of 1900. This is a superior campaign item. **$325**

The McKinley-Bryan battle for the presidency in 1896 is reflected in this well-decorated shot glass advertising Perry Buggies of Indianapolis. The glass, which is 2¾" high, bears the embossed images of McKinley and Bryan with the words "gold" and "silver" in circles above their heads. The glass also measures up to four tablespoons, and on the opposite side it measures liquor in terms of "ladies," "gentlemen," and, for those who demand more, there is a bas-relief likeness of a pig. Beneath the liquor side is the inscription, "Look for the puzzle." An unusual political keepsake, it's not easy to find. **$70**

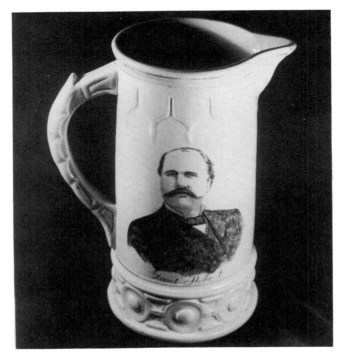

Covered glass mugs, which some believe actually served as mustard jars, were manufactured by the United States Glass Company in 1896 to promote the candidacies of both William McKinley and William Jennings Bryan. Attractively designed with a stipple finish, this one shows "Maj. Wm. McKinley" with the slogan "Protection and Prosperity." Well-molded with stippling and fancy trim, the 3½" mug shown here has the original cover, which adds about $12 to the price. The mugs still appear quite frequently in antiques shops, at shows, and in auctions, but prices are rising. **$55**

Two metal-topped canes showing pictures of the presidential and vice presidential candidates in the election of 1900 are treasured today by political collectors. The cane on the left shows the McKinley-Roosevelt ticket, while on the right are Bryan and his campaign mate, Stevenson. Both make interesting jugate souvenirs. Each **$125**

This McKinley plate was marketed for the 1896 campaign and shows McKinley's signature and the date beneath his portrait. The border is trimmed with fanciful touches of gold, and the transfer portrait is in reddish brown. Diameter, 7½". **$40**

This rare milk-glass jugate campaign plate shows in excellent bas-relief the 1900 presidential election candidates for the democrats William Jennings Bryan and Adlai Stevenson. Voters were familiar with both men, since Bryan had lost to McKinley in 1896 and Stevenson had served as vice president under Grover Cleveland after the election of 1892. The plate is heavy, with a well-defined floral leaf border. Attributed by glass historians Regis and Mary Ferson to the Indiana Tumbler and Goblet Company, Greentown, Indiana. Diameter, 8¼". **$250**

Because of her frail health, President McKinley was extremely thoughtful and considerate of his wife, Ida, pictured on this china plate which was one of a series of six made for the wives of the presidents. They were married in Canton, Ohio, on January 25, 1871. With the oval image of Mrs. McKinley in color, the plate, which bears an Imperial China marking, measures 6" × 6". **$20**

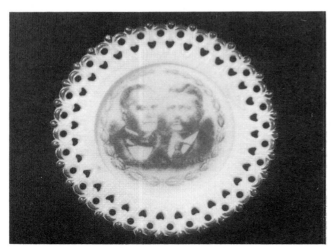

The McKinley-Roosevelt presidential ticket is pictured in a reddish brown transfer on this little milk-white campaign plate with a "one-O-one" border. The rim edging of the plate, manufactured in 1900, is green. Variations of coloring have been found, however, so the collector should not hold back on buying such a plate simply because the decorations are different. Often, the images of the candidates are faint. Diameter, 5¼". **$50**

William McKinley is immortalized in this white opaque glass statuette, which was also made in clear glass with a frosted finish. It was probably manufactured by the Canton Glass Company or the McKee Brothers. McKinley statuettes are scarce in either clear or milk glass and are believed to date from his first term in the White House. The statuettes have moderately well-defined features and are 5¼" high. **$165**

All the presidents through William McKinley appear on this tin serving tray distributed to promote the sale of shoes. The tray is highlighted by beautiful color and presents brief biographical data on all the presidents on the top and bottom rim. More than 17" long, the tray was made around 1900. **$175**

An unusual memento of the presidency of William McKinley is this sturdy, ornate napkin holder. The round focal point frames the celluloid-protected button image of McKinley and can be lifted up on one side for clamplike use as the result of a durable underside spring. The engraved design on the metal ring adds to the attractiveness of this complex little gadget. It is marked, "Pat. July 1900, J. Frame, Toledo, O." Length, 2¼". **$40**

President McKinley is pictured on this interesting cardboard fan which cooled the holder when pressure was applied to the wooden handle, causing the fan to spin one way and then another. The inset shows the Temple of Music at the Pan American Exposition in Buffalo, New York, where the president was shot. Strangely, the other side of the fan, decorated in graceful color, carries the slogan, "Welcome to Our Visitor." **$50**

A garland of flowers surrounds William McKinley's likeness on this heavy and somewhat different ceramic plate, which was possibly made after McKinley's assassination in 1901. Diameter, 9¼". **$40**

Richly colored old serving trays such as this one showing McKinley have been passed along in families. Many have holes near the top, from owners who used them as pictures to decorate their walls. An excellent presidential collectible measuring 16" in length. **$95**

A McKinley memorial bread tray quoting the president's deathbed comments was made after his assassination in 1901. The McKinley figure in the center of the tray closely resembles the McKinley image, with slight variations, that appeared on the gold standard tray made for the campaign of 1896. Birth and death dates have been added, and the tray has a wreath border. Still rather easily found, and often in the bargain category. Probably made by the United States Glass Company. Length, 10½". **$40**

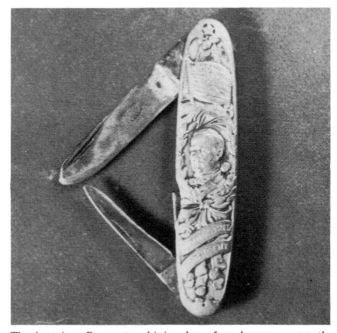

The American flag, a star shining down from heaven, a wreath around his head, flowers, and his most memorable, last quotation all are used to decorate this memorial jackknife honoring President McKinley. The three-bladed, 2¾" knife was made in Germany for "Our Martyred President." His deathbed quotation is on the reverse side. **$45**

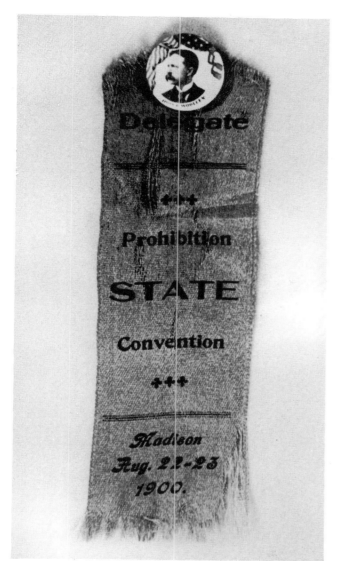

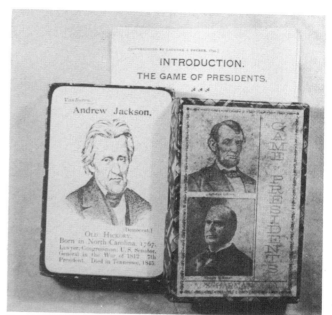

Parents have always believed that there's nothing wrong with a game that also helps their children to learn something. That was the case with this "Game of Presidents," sold after McKinley became the nation's chief executive in 1896. The cover pictures McKinley and associates him with the greatness of Abraham Lincoln. The card box is 3" × 4½", and the game was published by A. Flanagan of Chicago. **$20**

John G. Woolley was the presidential candidate for the Prohibition Party in 1900, the year McKinley won reelection. This attractive Woolley celluloid button and the blue-and-black ribbon are souvenirs of the Wisconsin State Prohibition Party convention held August 22–23, 1900, in Madison, Wisconsin. The well-worn ribbon is 6½" × 2". Ribbon, in condition shown **$20**; Button **$50**

McKinley's comments about having a little savings bank in the home are quoted on the side of this bank which was distributed by the State Bond and Mortgage Company. McKinley's picture and message appear on cardboard, which is framed by the metal edging. Size, 4¼" × 3¼". **$60**

This exceptionally attractive, 5" oval celluloid jugate with an easel back was made for the 1900 campaign by the Pin-Lock Medallion Company of Chicago. It pictures the tinted faces of the republican candidates, William McKinley and his runnning mate, Theodore Roosevelt. Scarce. **$290**

Among the brightly colored campaign posters made for McKinley and Roosevelt in 1900 is this one with the candidates are looking in opposite directions. It is 29" × 19½" in the gold frame, with the eagle, flags and candidates in full color. The slogan in blue across the bottom reads, "Protection-Prosperity-No Lowering of the Flag-Right-Justice-Honest Money-Full Dinner Pails-Our Country-Our Homes." What more could be said? **$275**

Youth still came through on the face of William Jennings Bryan in this jugate paperweight made for the campaign of 1900. Pictured with Bryan is his running mate, Adlai Stevenson. The heavy rectangular weight is 4¼" × 3" in size. **$80**

After McKinley's assassination, this blown-glass memorial tumbler appeared on the market. It pictures a view of McKinley facing to his right with the wording, "Our President, 1897 to 1901." Height, 3¾". **$50**

Among the scarce presidential campaign items from William McKinley is this unusual lacy milk-glass plate, which features a photograph of McKinley under a round center layer of clear glass. The oval picture is framed with blue paint, which has chipped under the clear glass. The outer rim of the portrait area is decorated with gold. The diameter of the plate, believed made in 1900, is 8¼". **$125**

1896 Presidential Election

$15 $30 $20

$20 $25 $10 $20

$20 $10 $10 $12

$ 8 $ 7 $10 $10

$25

$ 8 $ 8

$10 $ 9

$80

$35 $25 $22 $10 $70

$25 $10 $12 $15

$ 8 $10 $12 $10

$25 $50 $25 $ 9

$20 $40 $25

$60

$175 $15 $15 $20

$30 $12 $150

$30

$30 $50

$45

1900 Presidential Election

$45 $40 $40 $50

$18 $18 $15 $18 $18

$15 $15 $15 $12

$40 $50 $30 $30

$35 $30 $35

McKINLEY AND ROOSEVELT PROSPERITY PARADE CLEVELAND NOV. 3RD 1900.

$50

$20 $20 $18 $10 $10 $10 $ 8

$15 $15 $18 $20 $20

$35 $25 $35 $35 $30

$35 $40 $40 $35

$45 $100 $45 $50

$35 $65 $60

$45 $45 $75

$45 $40 $140

Theodore Roosevelt
1901–1909

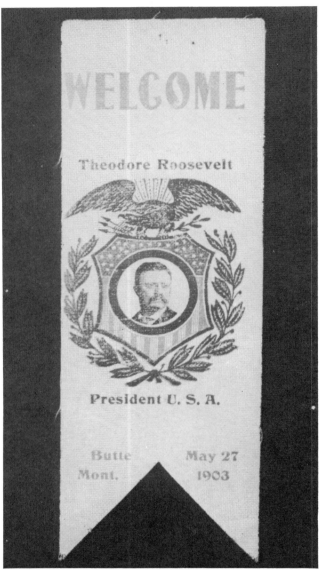

These ribbons were made for President Theodore Roosevelt's visit to Butte, Montana in 1903 and were distributed by the Montana Drug Company. The decorations and printing are in color. Length, 6¾". **$30**

Made by Wedgwood, this blue-and-white Theodore Roosevelt plate with a leafy border carries a reverse-side quotation from a speech given by the president in Syracuse, New York, in 1903. Old and desirable, this is a quality addition for the collector. Diameter, 9". **$65**

Teddy Roosevelt's political star was rising when this Rough Rider clock, showing him in full uniform astride his horse, was patented on April 25, 1899. The following year he was nominated as vice presidential candidate on the republican ticket. Before the end of 1901, because of William McKinley's assassination, he had become president. The clock is a Seth Thomas. Height, 10½". **$120**

Theodore Roosevelt's background as a Rough Rider was exploited to help him rise in politics. Here he's shown, sword raised, thundering along on his horse—presumably up San Juan Hill. The tin serving tray is 16" long. **$110**

Alton Brooks Parker and Henry Gassaway Davis were the democratic hopefuls in the 1904 democratic campaign to defeat Theodore Roosevelt and his vice presidential partner, Charles Warren Fairbanks. The Parker-Davis team is pictured on this jugate paperweight, with the shield and flags in color. Length, 4", width, 2½". **$85**

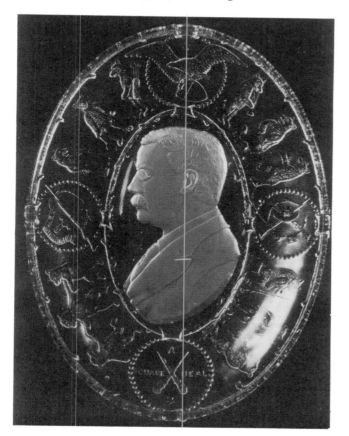

Americans liked the fact that Teddy Roosevelt spared the life of a little bear on a hunting trip and responded to scores of items that featured the teddy bear theme. This one shows Roosevelt kneeling next to a tree stump, which is being climbed by a bear. It's titled, "Teddy and the Bear." Made of china, it stands 3½" tall. **$65**

One of the brightest and most unusual glass trays made for the political field is the oval bread tray manufactured by the United States Glass Company for the campaign of 1904. It shows the frosted image of Roosevelt, wearing his pince-nez. The central portrait is surrounded by a delightful border that pictures teddy bears, his Rough Rider paraphernalia, the eagle and shield, and his slogan, "A Square Deal." The slogan is decorated with crossed clubs, presumably to indicate Roosevelt's policy of carrying "a big stick." The edge of the border is made to resemble a twig. Fortunately, these trays, which are 10¼" long, still come onto the market—but the prices are rising. **$135**

This Teddy Roosevelt watch fob was used during the campaign of 1904 when he ran with Charles Fairbanks. Rather common, its size is 1⅜". **$20**

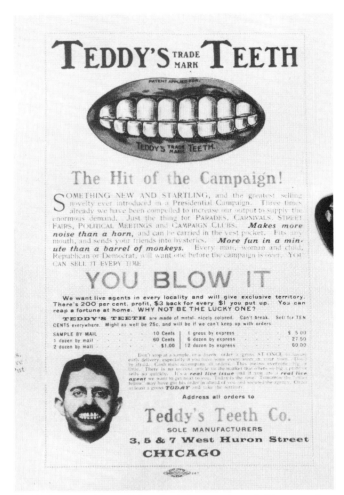

Teddy Roosevelt's teeth inspired the creation of this campaign noisemaker, described by the Chicago manufacturer as "more fun in a minute than a barrel of monkeys." Made of colored metal, the item was actually a horn so political activists could whoop it up for their candidate. Back in Teddy's day, these noisemakers sold for ten cents each. Today they are considerably more valuable. **$95**

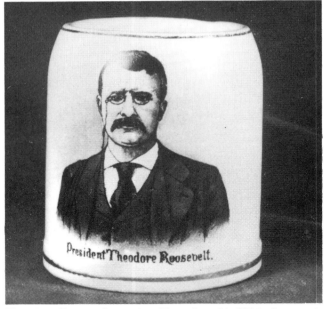

Theodore Roosevelt was in office when this 3⅛-inch ceramic mug, showing the president in full color, was made in Germany. Gold striping decorates the top and bottom of the mug, and the country of origin is stamped in red on the bottom. **$65**

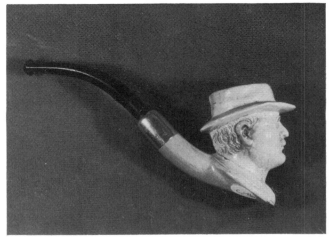

Theodore Roosevelt, garbed in his Rough Rider hat, is shown in this charming figural pipe, probably a campaign item dating from 1904. The pipe is 5¼" long. **$90**

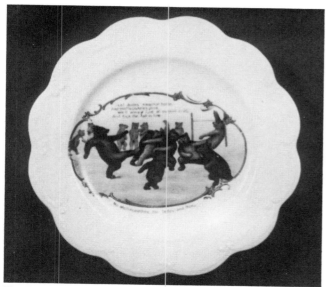

The Roosevelt bears always seemed to be having a whale of a time when Teddy Roosevelt was in the White House. This little plate with scalloped border shows the bears engaged in a game of football while, as the verse says, the "dudes remain at home." The transfer is in color. Diameter, 5½". **$55**

It takes a steady hand to put the white teeth in Teddy Roosevelt's mouth in this little presidential skill game. The teeth are tiny white balls that roll freely, and it doesn't take much of a wiggle to send them careening in the wrong direction. The face is in color, the rim is metal, and there's a mirror on the reverse side. Made during Roosevelt's years in the White House. Diameter, 2¼". **$170**

Made for his Bull Moose campaign in 1912, Teddy Roosevelt's likeness is impressed in copper mounted in a wooden frame. A similar brass plaque also was produced for Woodrow Wilson. Size, 6½" × 4¾". **$48**

Highlights in the life of Theodore Roosevelt are dramatized in rim scenes on this popular Rowland & Marsellus Company blue-and-white plate made in Staffordshire, England. Sold at the time that Roosevelt held office, it is one of the basic additions to any presidential collection and is still a bargain. Diameter, 10". **$50**

The entire Roosevelt family is identified on this little aluminum pin-tray with decorated corners. The group includes, in addition to President Teddy Roosevelt and Mrs. Roosevelt; Archibald; Theodore, Jr.; Kermit; Alice; Quentin; and Ethel. Size, 6¼" × 4¼". **$25**

An interesting story might be told by this delicate little punch cup, made by Bloomingdale's of New York and neatly etched, "President Roosevelt, 1902, Oyster Bay." Fine crystal, fit for a presidential party. Height, 2½". **$75**

Teddy Roosevelt looks out at the drinker from the side of this scarce glass flask made for the 1900 election, when he was the running mate of William McKinley. The flask has two tops, with the larger one, shown left, serving as the handy "shot" container. The reverse side of the flask has the embossed image of the American eagle. Height, 5½". **$190**

Just about every man of even modest means carried a pocket watch back in the early 1900s, so watch fobs were popular as campaign items. This one shows the embossed image of Theodore Roosevelt and emphasizes on the links "Trade follows the Flag" and "Protection, Prosperity and Panama." An elephant marked "GOP" is on the top link. The item is 6" long. **$45**

Nonpartisanship for the sake of sales is shown in this photo of a rather worn top of a cigar box. It's from 1904, when voters could take their choice of either Teddy Roosevelt or Alton Parker. **$8** (in condition shown)

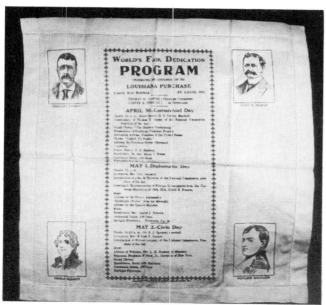

When they held the dedication ceremonies for the World's Fair in St. Louis in 1904, President Theodore Roosevelt was on the program. Another president, Thomas Jefferson, also was honored in observance of the Louisiana Purchase. The 17" × 17" textile shown here recalls the dedication and also pictures Roosevelt and Jefferson. **$45**

Designed by Eric Foster and inspired by the patriotic fervor of the nation's Bicentinnial, this frosted Theodore Roosevelt bust was made by the L. E. Smith Glass Company of Mount Pleasant, Pennsylvania. Along with others of George Washington, Thomas Jefferson, and Abraham Lincoln, also designed by Foster, the Roosevelt bust now has become a presidential collectible. The base carries Roosevelt's birth and death dates. Height, 5⅝". **$60**

The Rough Rider image never hurt Theodore Roosevelt at the polls, and it's reflected again here in an iron bank. Popular with collectors, the bank is 5" high. **$150**

It was Teddy Roosevelt who said that he was throwing his hat in the ring, and some enterprising bandanna-maker went out and produced a campaign textile stressing the message. Roosevelt's hat is shown in a center ring on this red-and-white bandana with the initials TR and caricatures of Roosevelt used for decorations. The size is 19¾" × 18". **$50**

Teddy Roosevelt always looked good on a cover, as demonstrated by these two examples. At left he is shown on the cover of a booklet for a local dry goods store, circa 1905. The Progressive Party song book at the right is a campaign piece from 1912 when Roosevelt ran as a Progressive. The jugate cover of the song book shows him with running mate Hiram Johnson. Each booklet is approximately 8" long. Advertising booklet **$15**; Progressive booklet **$35**

1904 Presidential Election

$15 $40 $10 $ 8 $25 $75 $20

$140 $80 $80 $80 $85

$45 $80 $300

$45 $45 $45 $35 $35

$45 $40 $45 $75 $35

$40 $25 $35 $30 $25 $15 $25

$160 $90 $140 $110 $90

$80 $75 $40 $75 $40

$50 $45 $50 $50 $45

129

$250 $45 $80 $60

$90

$175

$200 $75

$75 $60 $90

William Howard Taft
1909–1913

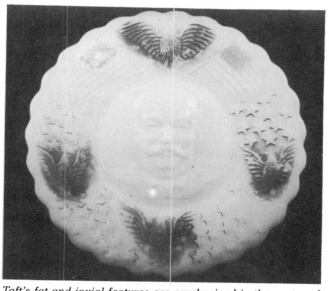

Taft's fat and jovial features are emphasized in the center of this 1908 campaign plate. Made of milk glass and decorated with a patriotic border showing eagles, flags, and stars, the plate became a favorite of those voters who believed that Taft was the right man to succeed Teddy Roosevelt. The diameter of the plate, produced in conjunction with another honoring William Jennings Bryan, is 7¼". **$65**

Bryan's third try for the presidency in 1908 is remembered by this milk-glass plate molded in bas-relief, with a similar plate made for the candidacy of William Howard Taft. Flags, stars, and eagles decorate the border. Although they are offered for sale only infrequently, the price on these plates has remained reasonable, and they therefore make good additions to either a milk glass or presidential collection. Diameter, 7¼". **$65**

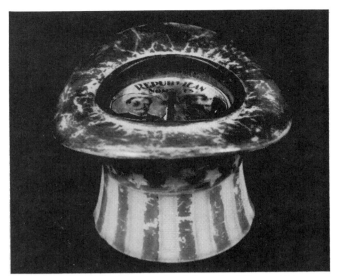

An Uncle Sam hat milk-glass bank in red, white, and blue was made for the nominees in the 1908 presidential election. This one features the republican candidates, William Howard Taft and James S. Sherman. The slotted tin closure on these little banks was topped by paper pictures of the nominees, with some showing just the man running for president. When circulated, the campaign hats were filled with candies. Many of the paper photos were torn when children later used the banks to save pennies. Height, 2½". **$75**

This jugate campaign tumbler shows William H. Taft "For President" and James S. Sherman "For Vice President;" it was made in 1908 to promote the republican candidates. Height, 3½". **$70**

This "Our choice" campaign plate for 1908 shows William Howard Taft and features gold trim on the edge and "Carrollton China" on the back. Diameter, 8½". **$40**

Matching campaign ribbons were made for the presidential election of 1908, with Taft facing Bryan. Collectors like to find them in pairs, such as this. The flags are red, white, and blue while the images of the candidates are in a brownish hue. The ribbons are 6" × 1⅞". Each **$30**

A twinkle of humor seems to be in the eyes of William Howard Taft in this plate, a companion piece to the Sevres campaign issue that also produced a plate for candidate William Jennings Bryan. The well-done transfer image of Taft is reddish brown, and the plate has a gold floral border. Diameter, 8". **$48**

The "Smiling Bill" and "Sunny Jim" plates made for the successful candidates in the 1908 election have become popular collectors' items. This octagonal, green- and gold-edged plate decorated with flowers shows Taft at the left with Sherman, his vice president. Both men seem to be enjoying themselves. The little banner between them carries the message, "An Invincible Combination." The plate measures 7" across. **$65**

Fine-quality Sevres plates were produced for the campaign of 1908. This one shows William Jennings Bryan, who at that time was about to suffer his third presidential defeat. This is an excellent likeness of an aging Bryan, with an attractive gold floral border. Diameter, 8". **$48**

Scarce political glass bread-trays were made for the republican and democratic candidates for the election of 1908. This one pictures the republicans, W. H. Taft and J. S. Sherman, along with the GOP elephant and with the American eagle on a shield. Taft and Sherman are described as "Our Candidates" on most of these trays, but this one says "Our Presidents," indicating that the mold was changed after their election. An excellent presidential memento, more than 11" long. **$185**

Presidential postcards decorated with cloth were made for the campaign of 1908. Here are two of them, with Teddy Roosevelt doing a selling job for William Howard Taft on the left, and William Jennings Bryan holding a balloon made of cloth while talking to the democratic donkey on the right. Scarce. Each **$55**

Taft and Sherman, the Grand Old Party duo in 1908, are shown on this attractive little tin campaign tip-tray. It has excellent color for the candidates, flags, White House, and trim. The rim of the 4¼" tray lists all the republican presidential nominees from 1856 on. Scarce. **$55**

William Howard Taft is honored in this attractive Bennington-type 10½" high bust. The brown and black shadings are covered with a high glaze. A fine display piece, it's not easily found. **$250**

This jugate plate, showing William Howard Taft and James S. Sherman, was a Staffordshire product imported by the Rowland & Marsellus Company of New York. Shown around the rim are key Washington, D.C. buildings, Mount Vernon, and the Washington Monument. It's a fine blue-and-white plate of historic significance. Diameter, 10". **$60**

William Howard Taft, looking dapper with a handlebar mustache, is glorified in this fancy-stemmed pipe made by Gambier of Paris. Taft is identified by his name on one side of the pipe. The facial features, hair, and mustache are extremely well done. The pipe is 7" long. **$90**

One of Taft's nicknames was "Billy Possum," so of course there were cartoons, postcards, and other items linking him to that identification. This scarce little metal child's mug, with its silverplate all worn off, shows Billy Possum wearing a cap and carrying a set of golf clubs, since Taft enjoyed golf for his much-needed exercise. The bottom marking shows this to be quadruple plate of the Eureka Silver Company, U.S.A. Height, 2½". **$100**

Watch fobs were distributed in abundance during the first decades of this century. This one was a campaign item for William Jennings Bryan in 1908. For the third time, voters decided that they didn't want Bryan to use whatever key he might have had to the White House. The fob is 1¾" long. **$25**

When time for summer vacation came, teachers used to give their students little souvenirs to remind them of the importance of a good education and hard work. This one was distributed in Crawford County, Wisconsin, in 1911. The well-designed, full-color cover shows all the presidents through Taft in the border. The back cover pictures the log cabin "Birthplace of Abraham Lincoln." Length, 5¾". **$20**

William Howard Taft is shown here in the form of a toby jug, made in Germany for sale in Washington, D.C. gift shops and elsewhere at the time Taft was in the White House. Taft's rosy cheeks and smile make this a pleasant little memento to place on a shelf in anyone's presidential collection. Height, 5". **$75**

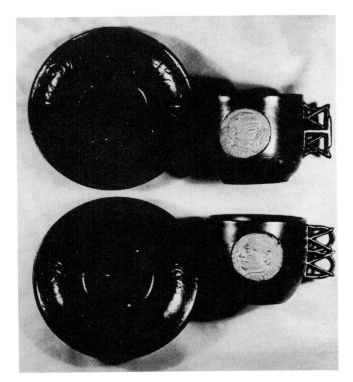

This rare combination of ceramic cups and saucers marks the 1908 presidential race between Taft and Bryan. The bas-relief images of Taft and Bryan appear on the side of the cups and are not glazed. Their names and the year also are shown. But what's more remarkable is that the handles on these little cups represent the initials of each candidate. The faces of the saucers also carry the names of the candidates and the year. Campaign items in every sense of the word, these make a great combination for collectors. Made in Waterloo, Iowa, the cups are 2½" high and the saucers have a diameter of 4¾". Pair **$200**

Animal symbols of the parties were made showing the candidates on celluloid buttons. Here we see the GOP elephant with the picture of Taft. The democratic choice, Bryan, was featured on the side of an iron donkey. The elephant is 6¾" long and 4¾" high. **$200**

136

1908 Presidential Election

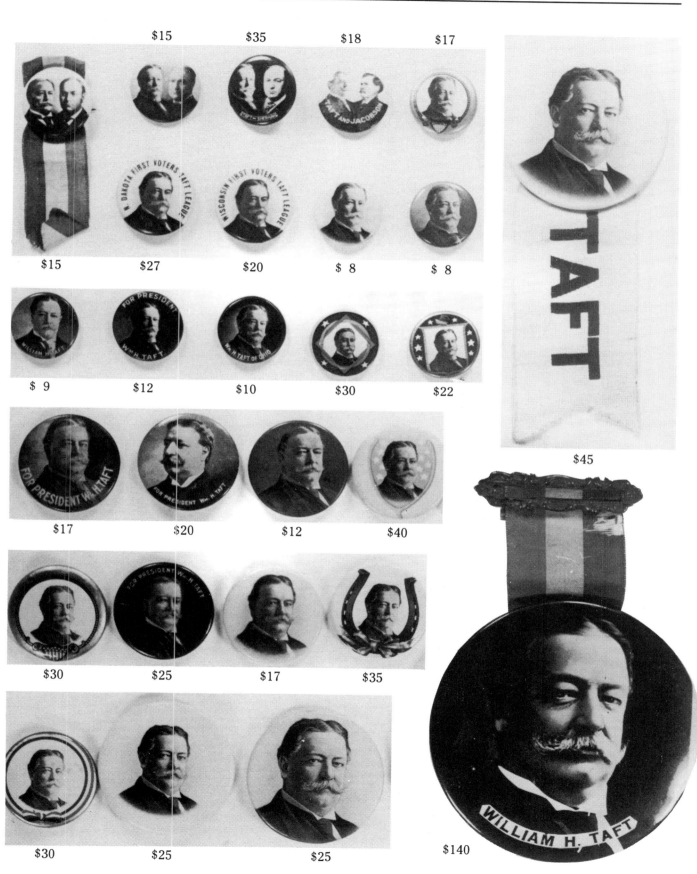

$15 $35 $18 $17

$15 $27 $20 $ 8 $ 8

$ 9 $12 $10 $30 $22

$17 $20 $12 $40

$30 $25 $17 $35

$30 $25 $25

$45

$140

$35 $20 $20 $17 $10 $25

$12 $10 $12 $10 $15 $30

$12 $30 $22 $25 $40

$250 $40 $40 $45 $35

$40 $40 $30 $175

$200 $250

$30 $35 $20 $20

Woodrow Wilson
1913–1921

A handsome historical reminder of the days of Woodrow Wilson, this heavy metal-art glass lamp has a shade made of caramel slag glass shaped like the Liberty Bell. The bell shade is topped by an impressive likeness of the American eagle. The base pictures an embossed image of Wilson in an oval setting, surrounded by sculptured impressions of U.S. doughboys in battle. The base is embossed "Phoenix-Milwaukee." An unusual lamp of good quality and made during World War I, it stands 16" high. **$225**

The Panama Canal is featured on this presidential plate, which was produced at the time Woodrow Wilson was in office. The geography shows the course of the Canal, and the border pictures all the American presidents through Wilson. The American shield and the flag background add richness to the flow blue-type coloring. Diameter, 8¼". **$30**

President Wilson has a place of honor next to Polish hero Thaddeus Kosciuszko on this full-color framing. Kosciuszko fought with American forces during the Revolutionary War and was a leader in the fight for Polish independence. The display dates from Wilson's presidency. **$40**

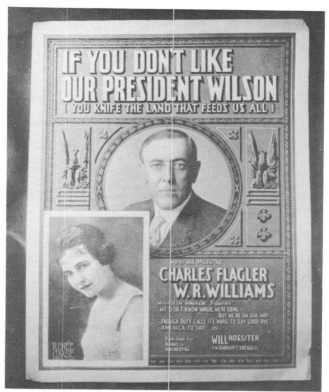

Patriotic support for President Wilson was the overriding theme of this song written during the World War I era. Finding sheet music honoring the presidents has become popular with collectors. **$20**

Little china plates adorned with his picture were made while President Woodrow Wilson was in the White House. Today these plates are desirable collectibles. The transfer image of Wilson is the same one that is used on china match holders. The diameter of the plate is 5". **$45**

This match holder, bearing the brownish transfer picture of Woodrow Wilson on both sides, probably was a giveaway at the time Wilson was in office. The flat-back china piece is decorated with two 4-leaf clovers and an advertising message that reads, "We appreciate your trade, P. H. Luecke & Co., Giddings, Texas." This item is growing increasingly hard to find. Height, 2". **$48**

Woodrow Wilson occupied the nation's highest office when this presidential plate was circulated. The White House is shown in color, with all the presidents through Wilson joined in oval portraits around the border. Usually found with much crazing, but a desirable plate, nonetheless. Diameter, 9⅝". **$50**

The presidency of Woodrow Wilson is recalled in this little Washington, D.C. souvenir match holder. Wilson and the White House are pictured in color under celluloid on one side, with a bright blue sky over the Capitol on the other. Size, 2¾" × 1½". **$50**

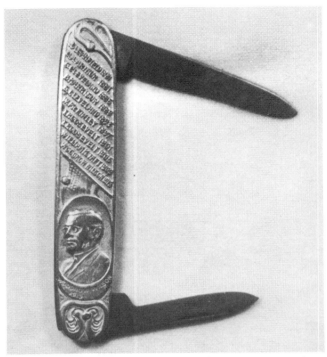

Jackknives have been campaign items for many years and are still being made. This one was made to honor Woodrow Wilson after his election in 1912. It carries the names and inauguration years of every president through Wilson. It was made in Germany. With both blades closed, the jackknife is 3⅜" long. **$35**

Support for President Wilson during World War I was the patriotic theme of this tin-framed wall hanging. The length of the frame is 5½". **$20**

Collectors who can afford the rarities join in on the bidding whenever this 6" button comes on the market—which isn't often. With a red border quoting "Undiluted Americanism," the button pictures Charles Evans Hughes who lost to Wilson in a close election in 1916. Hughes had not sought the presidential nomination, but it was his belief that no one had "the right to decline it." He lost to Wilson by 580,000 popular votes. History will remember him best as an outstanding jurist who served as the nation's eleventh Chief Justice. **$4,200**

This plaster bust of Woodrow Wilson was made by Mooseheart students in Mooseheart, Illinois, as indicated on the bottom. Wilson's name in signature form is shown on the front of the base, and on the back there's the quotation, "The world must be made safe for Democracy." Height, 6". **$30**

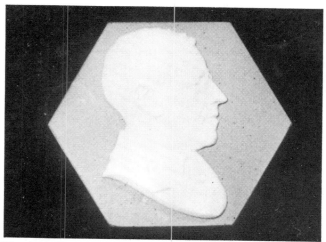

Woodrow Wilson is well portrayed in this attractive blue-and-white tile made by the Mosaic Tile Company of Zanesville, Ohio. Good detail, it measures 3" high × 3½" wide. **$40**

This World War I paperwight refers to "The War for Democracy, 1917" and pictures a vigorous-looking President Woodrow Wilson amid eagle and flag decorations in color. Length, 4¼"; width, 2¾". **$45**

Woodrow Wilson and his vision of world peace caught the imagination of much of the world, even though he did not achieve his goals. Here he is glorified in French on a little metal matchbox holder. Size, 2½" high. **$28**

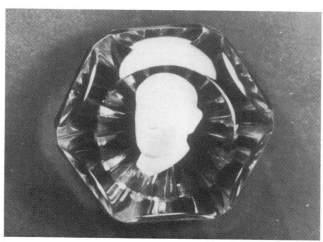

President Wilson was among the chief executives immortalized in modern Baccarat paperweights. The quality of this famous old French firm's production is superb, and at least one Baccarat presidential weight belongs in a diversified collection. **$85**

1912 Presidential Election

$35

$45 $45 $45 $45

$45 $15 $16 $10

$45 $35 $35 $40

$55

$25 $25 $7 $8 $12 $250

$15 $15 $12 $17 $10 $250

$25 $60 $20 $8 $10

$40 $40 $40 $60

$40 $30 $35 $40

$40 $40 $30 $30

$15 $8 $8 $12

$6 $7 $7

$18 $12 $10 $10

$200

(Mirror) $250

145

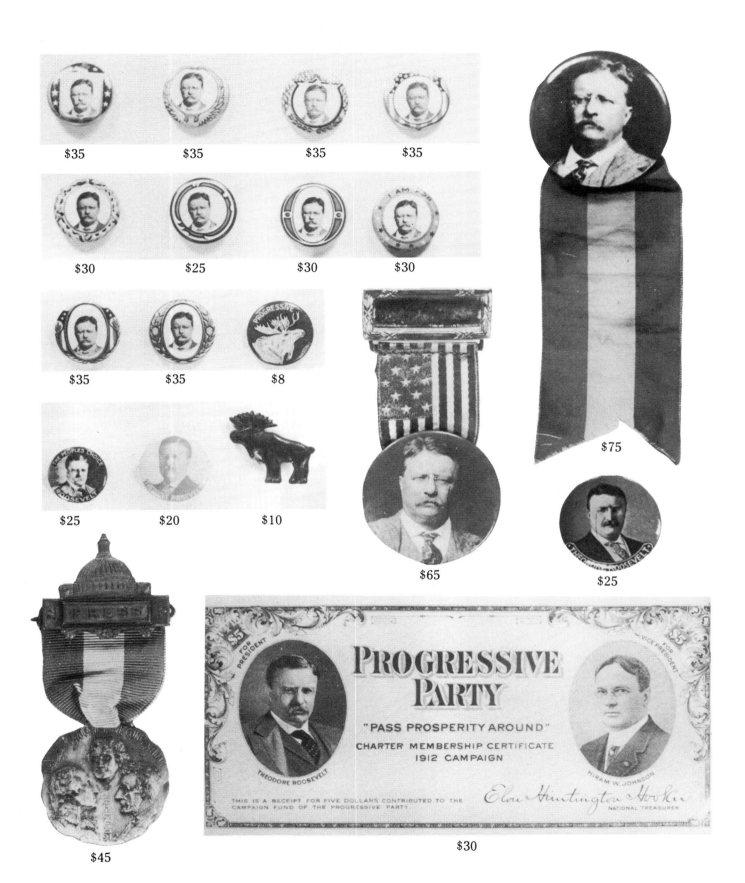

$35 $35 $35 $35

$30 $25 $30 $30

$35 $35 $8

$25 $20 $10

$65

$75

$25

$45

PROGRESSIVE PARTY
"PASS PROSPERITY AROUND"
CHARTER MEMBERSHIP CERTIFICATE
1912 CAMPAIGN

THEODORE ROOSEVELT   HIRAM W. JOHNSON

THIS IS A RECEIPT FOR FIVE DOLLARS CONTRIBUTED TO THE
CAMPAIGN FUND OF THE PROGRESSIVE PARTY.

NATIONAL TREASURER

$30

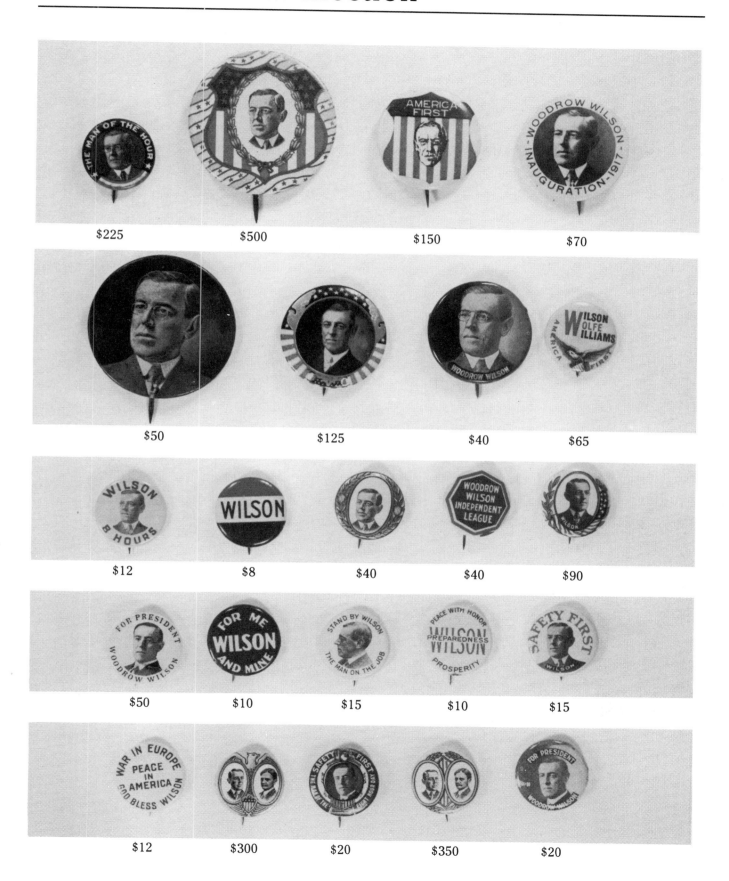

$225 $500 $150 $70

$50 $125 $40 $65

$12 $8 $40 $40 $90

$50 $10 $15 $10 $15

$12 $300 $20 $350 $20

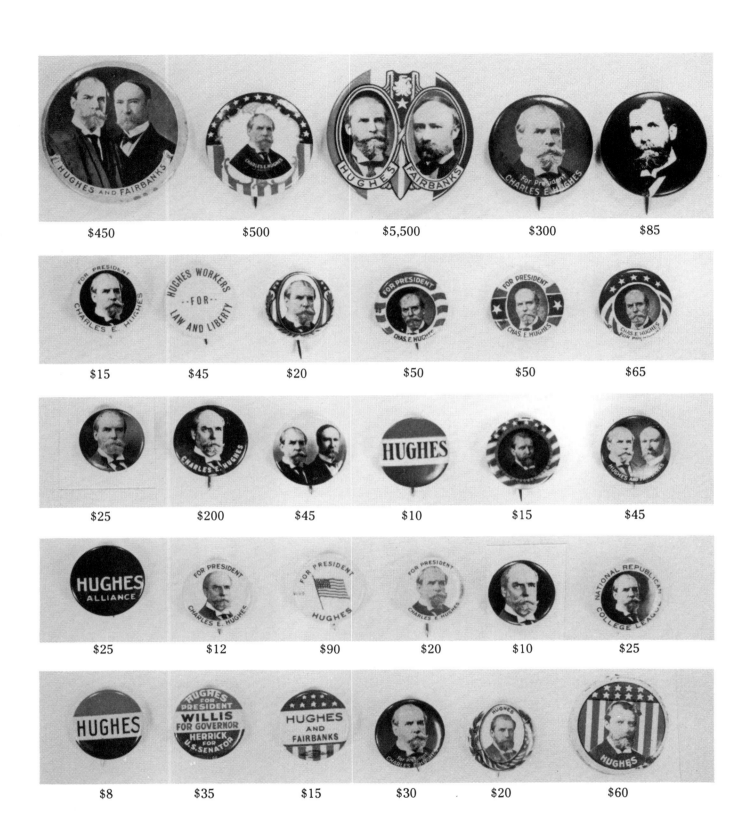

$450 $500 $5,500 $300 $85

$15 $45 $20 $50 $50 $65

$25 $200 $45 $10 $15 $45

$25 $12 $90 $20 $10 $25

$8 $35 $15 $30 $20 $60

$25 $25 $25 $12

$30 $20 $30

$20 $50 $100

$275

$125 $30 $65

$45 $30 $40

$35

$45

$300

Warren G. Harding
1921–1923

Eugene Debs, a labor union leader who founded the Social Democratic Party of America in 1897, ran as the presidential candidate of the Socialist Party five times. The fifth time (1920) he sought the nation's highest office, he did so from prison, having been sentenced to a 10-year term in 1918 for opposing the war with Germany and violating the new Espionage Act. Despite his imprisonment, he received nearly 920,000 votes. Respected by many Americans, Debs was released on the order of President Harding in 1921 and died in 1926 just two weeks before his 71st birthday. The 5" metal statue above shows him in prison garb. **$90**

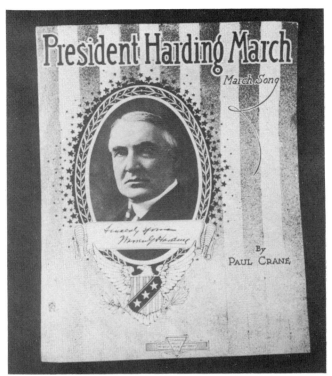

Songs have always been written to honor the presidents, and Warren Harding was no exception. Here's the "President Harding March," which has the usual flattering lyrics, including a line that reads "We have no cause for care, now that you're in the Presidential Chair." At that time, of course, no one could foresee Teapot Dome and Harding's problems with those he had trusted. **$25**

Laddie Boy, President Warren Harding's famous pet, is portrayed in this well-sculptured metal statue. (The statue also appears in the Color Section.) Held in Laddie Boy's mouth is a copy of the Marion Star. **$650**

James Cox for president and Franklin Roosevelt for vice president are recalled in this watch fob from the 1920 campaign. Above the oval portraits of the candidates is the wording "E Pluribus Unum," and at the bottom is the campaign slogan "Our Choice." The fobs are found with both a silver- and gold-plated finish and are not as scarce as another shield-shaped Cox-Roosevelt fob. The one shown here is 1½" long. $70

Warren Harding was in the White House when this 3" "souvenir penny of Kansas City" was made back in the early 1920s. An interesting presidential collectible. $35

When James Cox ran for president in 1920 on the democratic ticket with a vice presidential candidate named Franklin Roosevelt, the number of jugate buttons made was extremely limited—perhaps 70 at most. In 1981, a one-of-a-kind Cox-Roosevelt jugate sold for a record $33,000. The "Sunburst Eagle" design shown here, made by the St. Louis Button Company, also fared well, bringing $3,300. Because of their rarity, Cox-Roosevelt jugates in first-rate condition can be expected to bring even more in the future. $5,000

$100 $275 $225 $85

$250 $45 $110 $250

$45 $100 $550 $75 $60

$45 $35 $90 $9 $35

$60 $110 $20 $1,300 $150

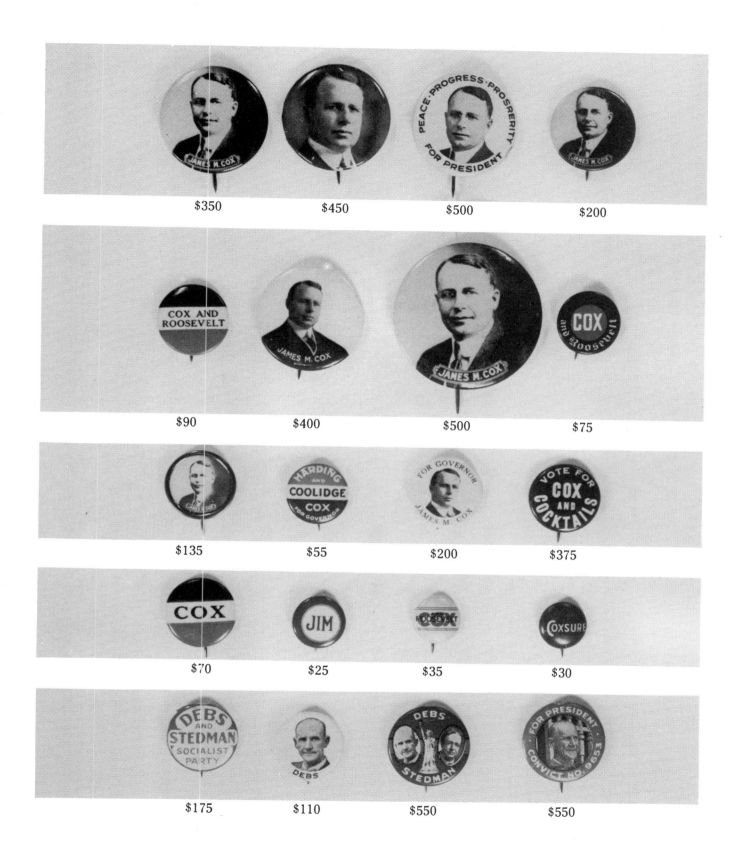

$350　　　　$450　　　　$500　　　　$200

$90　　　　$400　　　　$500　　　　$75

$135　　　　$55　　　　$200　　　　$375

$70　　　　$25　　　　$35　　　　$30

$175　　　　$110　　　　$550　　　　$550

UNDER
The 19th
Amendment
I CAST MY
FIRST VOTE
Nov.2nd,1920

Harding
Coolidge

The Straight
Republican
Ticket

Lancaster, Pa.

$125

DELEGATE

$40

$8 $8 $8 $60

$9 $6 $6 $500

$4 $4 $4 $4 $15

$500 $100

$130 $25 $25 $15

$70

PALMER

$65

154

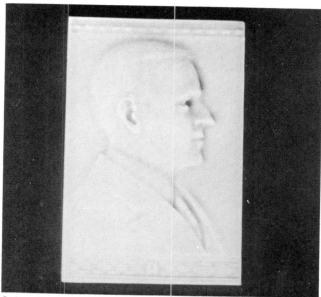

Calvin Coolidge appears on this light-blue tile made during the late 1920s when Coolige served as president. The name "Coolidge" in written form can be faintly discerned on Coolidge's left shoulder. The tile is 2⅞" wide and 4⅜" long. **$50**

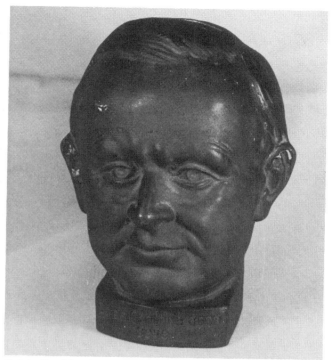

Calvin Coolidge had a reputation for thrift, so what better way to remember him than with a bank? Not too many of these brown-toned pottery banks have survived, and those still around are popular with presidential collectors. The little saying on the front of the base reads, "Do as Coolidge Does— Save." The money slot on the top of Coolidge's head was big enough for a silver dollar. However, to get the money out you had to break the bank—a tragedy in the eyes of today's collectors. Height, 5". **$125**

Finding much of anything from the 1924 presidential candidacy of John W. Davis isn't easy, so this little clear glass berry dish made by Hazel-Atlas Glass Company has become an important collectible. The dish, which has fluted sides, was made as a souvenir for a Davis rally in his campaign against Calvin Coolidge. Diameter, 4". **$65**

Grace Coolidge autographed this attractive lithograph of the White House, which is neatly framed under glass. It's a fine remembrance of a gracious first lady. The frame measures 7¼" × 4¾". **$50**

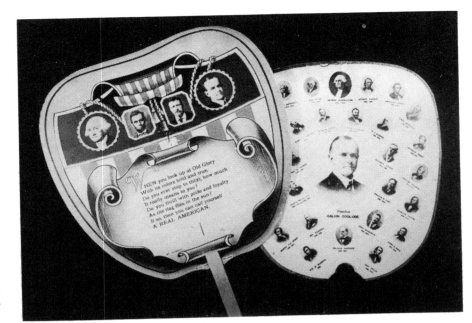

For his campaign slogan in 1924, the supporters of Calvin Coolidge used to say, "Keep Cool with Coolidge." And what better way to keep cool than with fans such as these. Both fans, stressing presidential themes, were made when Coolidge was in office. The one with Coolidge in the center is 7¼" wide while the other is 9" wide. Each **$15**

Calvin Coolidge was in the White House when this pencil box was made honoring our American presidents. The bottom of the box lists all the presidents along with the years they served. For Coolidge, the only year listed is 1924, when he was elected. Made by the Eagle Pencil Company of New York, the red box—familiar to many who went to school in the 1920s—is 11" long × 4" wide. **$25**

1924 Presidential Election

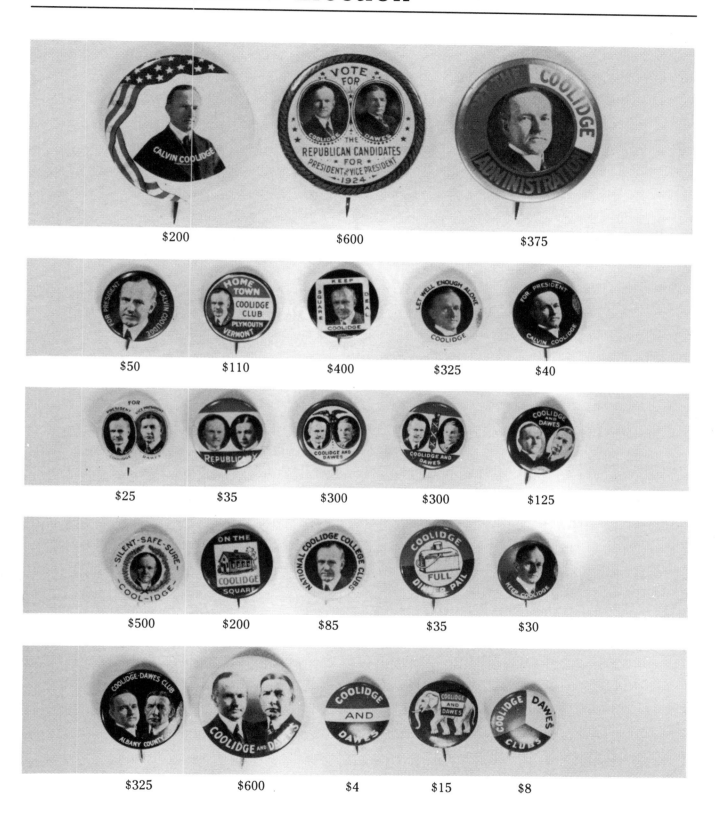

$200 $600 $375

$50 $110 $400 $325 $40

$25 $35 $300 $300 $125

$500 $200 $85 $35 $30

$325 $600 $4 $15 $8

$125 $125 $110 $500

$450 $125 $75 $85

$200 $90 $700 $110

$90 $1,000 $75 $150

$80 $45 $65 $60

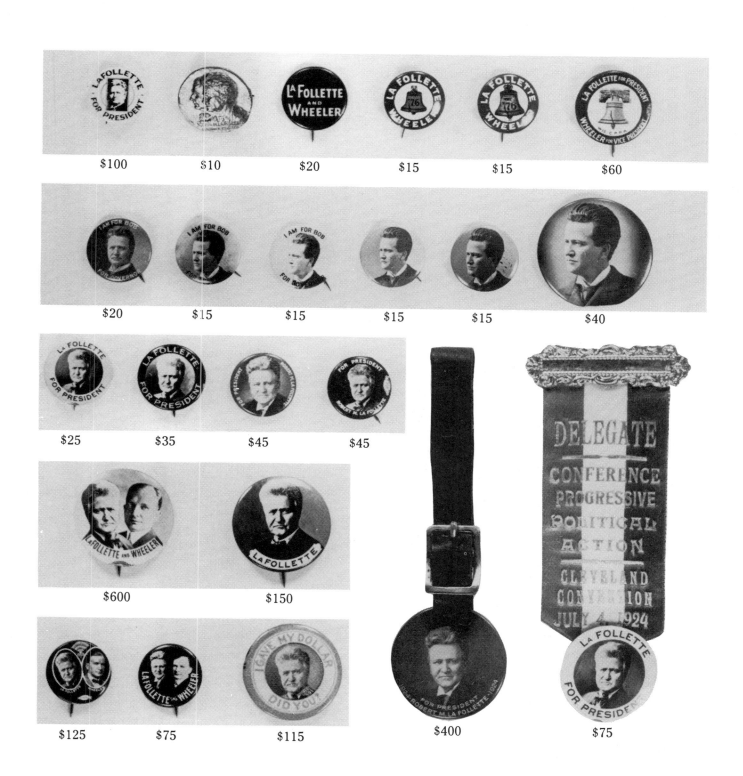

$100 $10 $20 $15 $15 $60

$20 $15 $15 $15 $15 $40

$25 $35 $45 $45

$600 $150

$125 $75 $115

$400 $75

Herbert Hoover
1929–1933

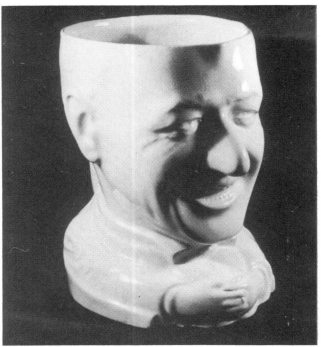

Alfred Smith, the Happy Warrior who lost to Herbert Hoover in the 1928 election, is the subject of this toby pitcher. Made under the Patriotic Products Association Gold Medal China label, the 7" pitcher is a companion to the Hoover toby. A popular campaign item, it's found less often than the Hoover pitcher. $65

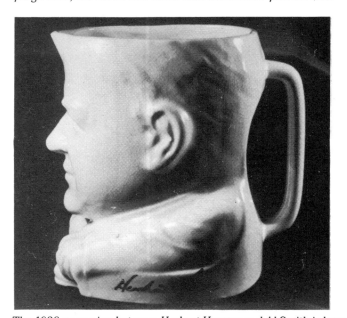

The 1928 campaign between Al Smith and Herbert Hoover led to the distribution of the souvenir metal busts pictured here. Nothing fancy, each is fairly well molded, with the candidates' names embossed on the center front. The busts are 4" high × 4¾" wide. Each $35

Even matchbook covers make good presidenial collectibles. This pair shows Alfred E. Smith featured on the left and the Herbert Hoover and Charles Curtis duo on the right. Many of these campaign boosters were circulated in 1928. Hoover-Curtis $30; Smith $20

The 1928 campaign between Herbert Hoover and Al Smith is brought to mind by this Hoover toby pitcher. The bottom has the shield label of the Patriotic Products Association and the words, "Gold Metal China, O. C. Co., Made in U.S., Patent Applied For." As in the case of the Smith toby pitcher, the facial likeness is skillfully done. Collectors who are lucky still find these tobies occasionally at flea markets and, more often, in shops. Height, 7". $65

When the ladies powdered their noses, they were reminded of the importance of their vote by this compact made for candidate Al Smith in the 1928 presidential election. The diameter is 2½". **$85**

The center medallion of this token-like, stacked paperweight pictures George Washington and President Herbert Hoover in bas-relief. Previous presidents and the years they took office are shown on the other "tokens." Width, 5¼". **$40**

This "Hoover for President" bumper attachment, made for the campaign of 1928 is painted blue and white on tin and measures 5¼" wide. **$15**

Hoover is pictured here on a wooden paperweight that was made around the time of his presidency. The angular-shaped weight is 3" high. **$30**

A second term was advocated in this old oilcloth tire cover made for the 1932 election. However, with the Depression deepening, voters had lost confidence in Hoover and turned to his democratic opponent, Franklin D. Roosevelt. The tire cover is an unusual and interesting memento of the campaign. **$165**

Shield plaques in rich colors on cardboard were made for the democratic and republican candidates in the 1928 presidential election. The GOP team of Herbert Hoover and Charles Curtis are shown at left, with the Happy Warrior, Al Smith, and his running mate, Joseph Robinson, on the right. The plaques are 7½" high. Hoover-Curtis $165; Smith-Robinson $150

This is a souvenir medal from Herbert Hoover's inauguration on March 4, 1929. The new president didn't know it then, but before the year was over the nation would be rocked by financial disaster on Wall Street. Length, 2¼". $35

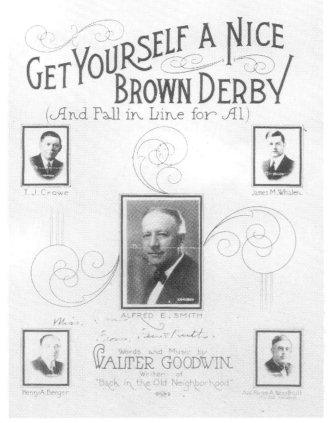

Those who supported Al Smith as a presidential candidate believed in keeping the voters singing. This sheet music is one of the examples, with the lyrics urging voters to get a brown derby and then "fall in line for Al." $8

1928 Presidential Election

$45 $20 $22 $20

$45 $5 $18 $15 $35

$7 $5 $4 $3 $5

$50

$4 $12 $2

$100 $125

$200 *(Holed for license plate attachment)*

SPECIAL OFFICER

$30

$6 $5 $4 $15

$8 $10 $15 $8

$55

FOR PRESIDENT
ALFRED E. SMITH

$100

$100

$25

FOR PRESIDENT
ALFRED E. SMITH

FOR
PRESIDENT
SMITH

Hello
Al.

$10 $25 $17

$35

FOR PRESIDENT
ALFRED E. SMITH

$150

$20

$85

$250 *(Holed for license plate attachment)*

$20 *(Needles packet, front and back)*

Franklin D. Roosevelt
1933–1945

Getting the nation back to work was the general theme stressed on this 1933 lampshade honoring the social programs of President Roosevelt. The shade shows a determined-looking Roosevelt, with decorations including the NRA symbol, a farmer at work in the fields, a train and a ship, and smoke coming out of busy factories. A hard-to-find item. The shade is 5" high. **$60.**

Canes were fine for promoting most presidential candidates, but for the handicapped Franklin D. Roosevelt, they certainly weren't appropriate. Yet this one was made for FDR's 1932 campaign. The other side of the handle says "For President," and shows the "32" date. The metal cane attachment is about 8" long. **$85**

"The New Deal" slogan and the embossed image of Franklin Roosevelt in a shield on the side of this tan-colored, barrel-shaped mug offer a variation of the happy days theme. It was made early in Roosevelt's presidency. Many collectors like to get a half-dozen or more of these and serve beer to their guests. Height, 4". **$15**

"Happy Days Are Here Again" is the theme of this beer-barrel-shaped green pottery mug with a heavy glaze. Made for the end of Prohibition when Franklin Roosevelt was in the White House. The slogans on such mugs always will be associated with memories of FDR. Height, 4¾". **$25**

Prohibition ended, "Happy Days" mugs were circulated early in the presidency of Franklin Roosevelt. This one is white, picturing a beer keg on one side and the words "Happy Days Are Here Again" on the other. The bottom is marked "General Beverage Sales Co." Height, 5". **$25**

After Franklin Roosevelt took control of the nation's destiny in the 1932 election, little metal statues of FDR began appearing in the stores. This one shows a young Roosevelt and carries the message, "Our New Deal President, Franklin D. Roosevelt, 1933." **$20**

One of the most commonly found reminders of the days of Franklin Roosevelt is this little "Happy Days" shot glass decorated with the democratic donkey. **$6**

Made of tin, this little "Happy Days" bank has found its way into many presidential collections. It's another reminder that Prohibition was repealed when Franklin Roosevelt came into office. Height, 4". **$8**

Franklin Roosevelt's smiling face in bas-relief peers out from the side of this fine Stangl Pottery pitcher, while the heavy brows of Roosevelt's first vice president, John Nance Garner, dominate the image on the matching mug. The pitcher is 7¼" high, and the mug is 4" high. All the items in this set bear the familiar "Happy Days Are Here Again" theme impressed on the reverse side of the faces. APIC member Fred L. Israel researched the set for an article in the "Political Bandwagon" publication and found that there are seven known mugs to go with the pitcher. He concluded that the set dates from the 1932 democratic convention when Garner, Al Smith, James Farley, William McAdoo, Albert Ritchie, Newton Baker and, of course, Roosevelt all played major roles in the convention. Pitcher $185; Each mug $40

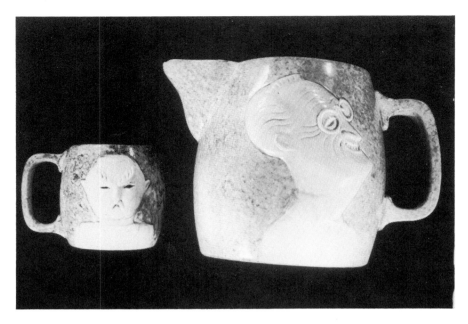

These little metal statues were popular during the Chicago World's Fair. Marked on the front "Franklin D. Roosevelt, 1933." Height, 4½". $20

Inexpensive metal lamps and clocks showing FDR at the helm as "The Man of the Hour" still are offered for sale frequently in shops and at flea markets. They were made during his first term. The lamp shown, with an apricot-colored globe, stands 16" high. $45

A companion piece for the large Franklin Roosevelt "Happy Days Are Here Again" pitcher is this barrel-shaped Stangl Pottery mug, embossed with FDR's confident likeness. Signed "Stangl" on the bottom. Height, 4". **$40**

Smoking his familiar cigar and smiling, Al Smith was one of the democratic superstars at the time of the 1932 presidential election. The Stangl mug shown here was part of a set that went with the large Roosevelt "Happy Days" pitcher. Height, 4". **$40**

Young and handsome, Franklin Roosevelt is pictured in full color on these wall plaques, probably made around the time that he took office. The large celluloid has a diameter of 9", while the other is 4⅝" × 3⅝". A black label shows that the large plaque was made by the P. N. Company of Chicago. Large **$50**; Small **$22**

A Franklin Roosevelt clock features the president in the stately company of Abraham Lincoln and George Washington. As with most of these items, FDR is at the helm. The grouping is titled, "Steersmen of U.S.A." The clock stands 12½" high. **$85**

Bookends and political pins are featured in this photo showing collectibles from Franklin Roosevelt. The iron bookends capture the profile image of Roosevelt along with one of his famous quotations, "There is nothing to fear but fear itself." The pins in the background are still on the store card. Marketed out of Giraid, Ohio during the Great Depression, the ¾" pins picture a smiling Roosevelt, who is described as "Your Friend." The bookends are 6⅜" high. Bookends **$55**; Pins, each **$20**

The National Recovery Act symbol can be seen on the lid of this Depression-era cigar box that was used to sell "Franklin D. Roosevelt" cigars. It seemed that the smiling face of FDR helped keep spirits up when the economy was down. **$20**

Wendell Willkie's acceptance speech on August 17, 1940, in Elwood, Indiana, is recalled in this red, white, and blue star-decorated tumbler, which also pictures the candidate. Height, 4½". **$18**

When these inexpensive clear glass tumblers were made to help promote the candidacy of Alfred M. Landon, the nation still was in the throes of the Great Depression. It was 1936, and a similar tumbler also was made for President Franklin Roosevelt. Delicate though they be, some of the campaign tumblers were saved and now are eagerly sought by political collectors. Height, 4⅝". **$45**

The dome on this heavy paperweight picturing President Franklin Roosevelt is 3" high and is decorated with a ring of colored canes. The base is blue, speckled with gold. A matching weight was made for Britain's Sir Winston Churchill, perhaps inspired by the winning combination of these two Allied leaders during World War II. **$100**

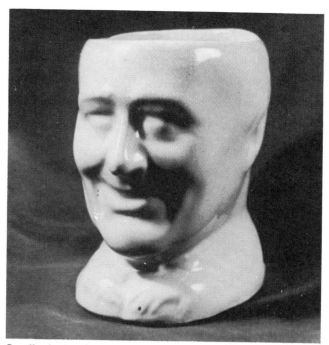

Small toby jugs made in the likeness of Franklin Delano Roosevelt are sought after by presidential collectors. Some are white; others are tan. These attractive ceramic souvenirs are 3¾" high. **$40**

"Life Begins in '40" was the slogan used frequently in 1940 when Wendell Willkie unsuccessfully tried to head off a third term for President Franklin D. Roosevelt. This plaster elephant carried the slogan on the base, with the word "Constitution" inscribed on the log the GOP elephant is holding with its trunk. The campaign elephants were made in 1939 in Green Bay, Wisconsin. **$35**

Those who wondered whether Franklin Roosevelt intended to break precedent and seek a third term received their answer in this amusing little hard-rubber FDR head nodder. The back of the campaign item asks the question, "Going to run for a third term?" For an answer, you set the rocker-like head on a table, then tap the chin. This sets the head to nodding about a dozen times in a definite "yes" manner. It's an interesting presidential memento. **$55**

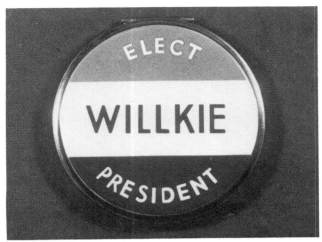

Wendell Willkie's bid to win the presidency in the 1940 campaign prompted the production of many promotional items, including this red, white, and blue compact with the slogan, "Elect Willkie President." The inside is marked "Volupte, U.S.A." Diameter, 3". **$35**

Words showing that he was ready for anything are featured on this little milk-glass campaign ashtray for 1940 GOP presidential candidate, Wendell Willkie. Diameter, 3½". **$12**

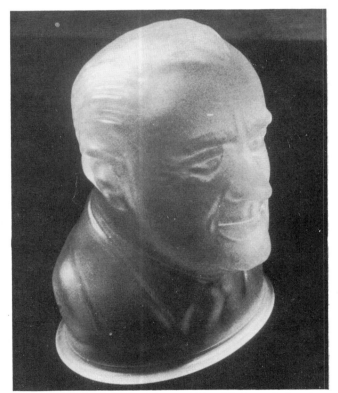

Large enough to be lighted from within, this frosted glass bust of Franklin Roosevelt is a somewhat eerie portrayal of our 32nd president. The bust stands 9" tall and has a 5" base. The facial features are not as fine as they might be, and the skin is not smooth. But in some respects, these differences only add interest. **$125**

Flags of the Allied nations are shown in color as a border decoration for this attractive plate honoring President Franklin Roosevelt. Although not marked on the back, the plate appears to have been made by the Salem China Company. Diameter, 10⅞". **$40**

A handsome gold-decorated border adds to the dignity of this fine souvenir plate picturing President Franklin D. Roosevelt. Large, with a diameter of nearly 11", the plate was made by the Salem China Company. The transfer image of Roosevelt is reddish brown. **$40**

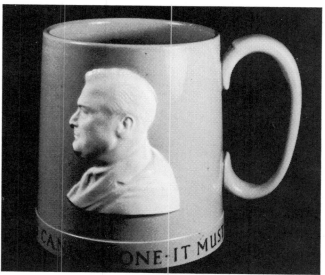

Franklin D. Roosevelt made many stirring speeches during his years in office, and this Wedgwood blue-and-white mug commemorates his words, "This can be done, it must be done, it will be done." The Wedgwood image of FDR, however, shows him to be somewhat heavier than most Americans remember. On the reverse side of the 4¼" high mug is the embossed symbol of an eagle. **$90**

A memorial tile of Franklin Roosevelt, 6" × 6", has a chronology of the important dates of his life on the reverse side. The dates are bordered in black and bear the name of the Kemper-Thomas Company, Cincinnati, Ohio. **$18**

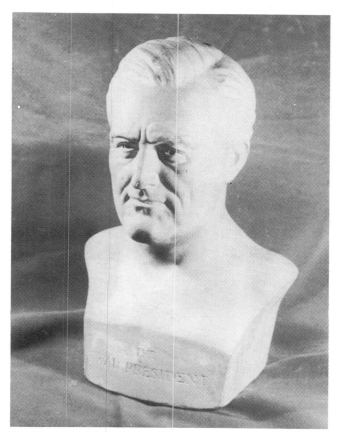

President Franklin D. Roosevelt looks young and strong on this heavy plaster bust entitled "The War President." The reverse side is marked. "To Hon. Frances Perkins, Miniature replica of bust of President Roosevelt, Presented to the People of the United States by the AHEPA." Frances Perkins served FDR for four terms as Secretary of Labor. The unusual statue is 10" high. **$30**

Franklin D. Roosevelt is the subject of this clear-glass bust candy container with a frosted finish. The features are reasonably accurate, and the hollow base helps create interesting facial shadows when the bust is placed in the light. It stands 5" high, and has "F. D. Roosevelt" embossed on the base. **$85**

An Indiana state democratic convention medal for delegates in 1946 honored the memory of Franklin D. Roosevelt with the message "Carry On." The same slogan had been used in Roosevelt's reelection campaign. The medal is 3¼" long. **$25**

This deep-green bottle with an almost carnival glass–type finish pictures a jaunty Franklin Roosevelt with a hat and a long cigarette holder jutting from his mouth. His name and the dates of his birth and death are on the front. On the reverse side is a quotation from a famous speech he made, the dates of his term in office, and his signature. This commemorative was made by the Wheaton Glass Company, Millville, New Jersey. Height, 7¾". **$18**

Looking youthful and strong, Franklin Roosevelt was honored on this fine presidential plate designed for wall display. The plate, which has a green wreath border and probably was made after his death, was manufactured in Holland. Diameter, 10⅜". **$65**

These two ashtrays were made with the likeness of President Franklin D. Roosevelt on them. The one on the left is a souvenir of Warm Springs, Georgia, site of "The Little White House;" the other was made in England. The round ashtray has a diameter of 5"; the square one is 4" × 4". Round **$12**; Square **$15**

1932 Presidential Election

$7 $12 $18 $25

$7

$8 $7 $5 $6 $6 $5

$25 $6 $4 $3 $3 $12

$30

$8 $20 $6 $12 $14 $6

$40 $90 $50

$30

$250 $55 $160

$225 $350 $30 $125 $110

$25 $65 $12 $12 $30

$25 $20 $20 $5 $5

$15 $5 $18 $30 $10

$40

$50 $75

$75

$175

$4 $15 $5 $4 $8 $9

$10 $12 $4 $12 $4 $5

$6 $7 $10 $25 $5 $35

$18 $6 $20 $5

$40

$30 $12

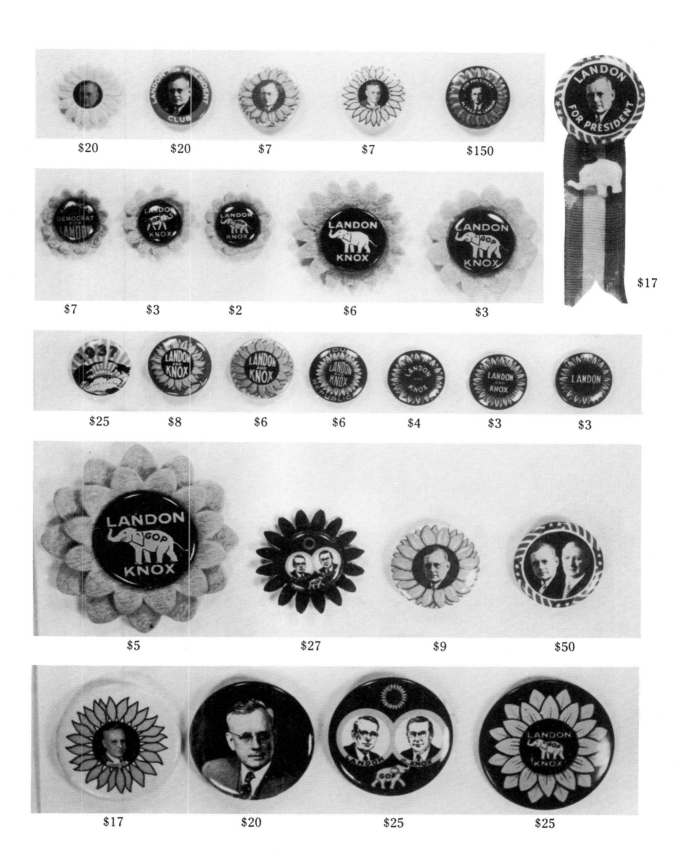

$20 $20 $7 $7 $150

$17

$7 $3 $2 $6 $3

$25 $8 $6 $6 $4 $3 $3

$5 $27 $9 $50

$17 $20 $25 $25

$50 $25

$35 $40

1940 Presidential Election

$12

$18 $50 $9 $25

$5 $5 $3 $3 $7 $17

$30 $7 $6

$35

$12 $5 $6

$8

$3

$6 $5 $6 $8

$10

$25 $18 $25 $25

NO CROWN FOR FRANKLIN   WILLKIE NOT ROYAL BUT LOYAL   TWO TIMES IS ENOUGH FOR ANY MAN   NO THIRD INTERNATIONALE THIRD REICH THIRD TERM

$6 $5 $5 $6

$10 $3 $2 $3 $5 $50

WIN WILLKIE WITH

NO THIRD TERM — VOTE REPUBLICAN NOVEMBER 5-1940

$25

$17 $10 $8

FOR PRESIDENT WILL-

$12

AMERICA'S HOPE

OUR NEXT PRESIDENT WENDELL L. WILLKIE

$20

$7 $8 $7

$200 $15 $8

OUR PRESIDENT

FRANKLIN D. ROOSEVELT

$35

OUR NEXT PRESIDENT

WENDELL LEWIS WILLKIE

$17

WILLKIE FOR PRESIDENT

$150

UP-ON AMERICA WIN WITH WILLKIE

$35

We Want F.D.R. Again

$12

LABOR RALLY
A. F. of L.-C.I.O.
Railroad Brotherhood

ROOSEVELT

$90

$2 $2 $3 $4 $6

$3 $3 $6 $2 $3 $5

$4 $5 $30 $10 $4 $7

$12 $6 $5 $9 $8

$18 $8 $20

$30 $7 $8 $8

$140 $5 $6 $5

$7 $8 $8

$32

$5 $4 $3 $3 $3

$4 $4 $2 $5 $2

$3 $3 $3

$17

$7

$12

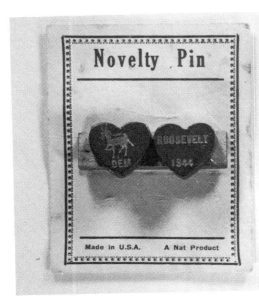

$15

$15

$15

$12

Harry Truman was a man who liked to keep busy, and he did so even after he returned to his home in Independence following his years in Washington. In a good strong hand, here's an autographed photo that is dated Dec. 12, 1953. The framing is 12" × 5". $200

They were waving pennants for a confident Thomas E. Dewey in 1948, but American voters responded instead to the "give 'em hell" campaign conducted by Harry Truman. Today the pennants are reminders of that colorful campaign. $22

The Capitol looms in the background on this tie made for Thomas Dewey's 1948 campaign against Harry Truman. $18

President Harry Truman is remembered in this pale-blue Wedgwood jasperware sweet dish made in England for the American market. The gutsy determination that people think of when they recall Truman is captured in the excellent facial detail. Diameter, 4⅜". **$15**

That famous Truman look is captured well on this souvenir-shop china from Washington, D.C. Truman plates usually attract the attention of collectors more readily than many of the others because mementos from his presidency are harder to find. Diameter, 7⅛". **$18**

1948 Presidential Election

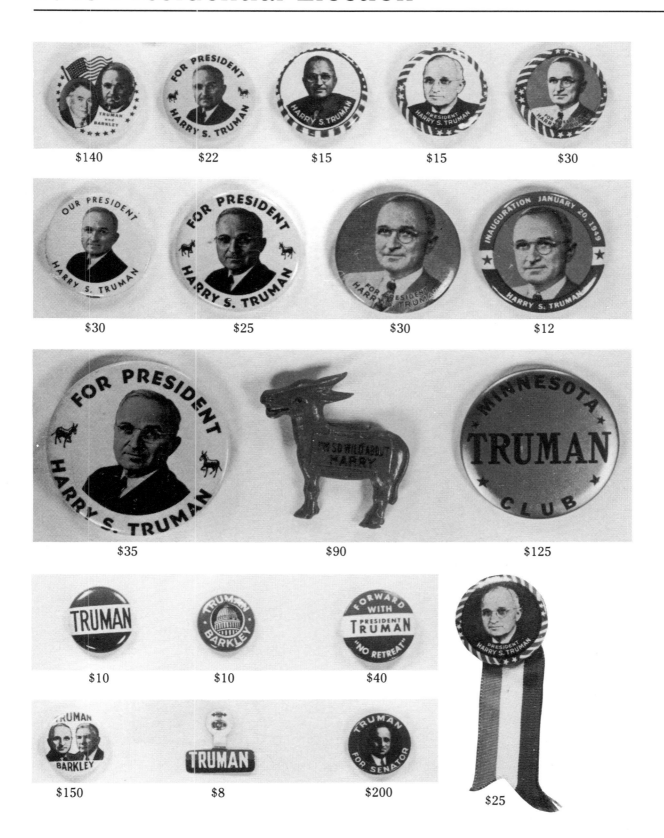

$140 $22 $15 $15 $30

$30 $25 $30 $12

$35 $90 $125

$10 $10 $40

$150 $8 $200 $25

$3 $8 $20 $25 $5 $4

$7 $6 $9 $15

$15 $12 $12

$3 $3 $3 $4 $3 $4

$8 $8 $25 $6 $8

$25 $15

$45 $30

$100 $45

Dwight D. Eisenhower
1953–1961

Neckties made for the 1952 presidential campaign pictured two republicans seeking the nomination, war hero General Dwight D. Eisenhower and United States Senator Robert Taft. Eisenhower was nominated on the first ballot and went on to serve two terms in the White House. Each **$20**

"I like Ike" was the battle cry for republicans during the campaign of Dwight D. Eisenhower. This tumbler carries the slogan and a decoration that emphasizes that Ike would best serve the interests of rural as well as urban voters. Height, 4¾". **$22**

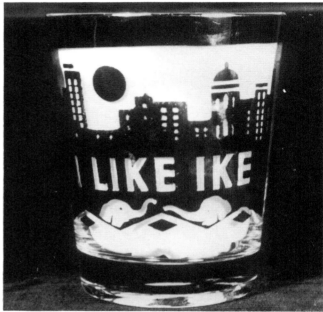

Eisenhower's winning smile has made this campaign bandanna popular with collectors. The coloring is red, white, and blue. These are still found at bargain prices. **$35**

A starred border decorates this attractive likeness of President Dwight Eisenhower commemorating his inauguration January 20, 1953. The reverse marking shows the plate was decorated by Delano Studios of New York. Diameter, 10⅝". **$22**

Whistle-stop campaigning is the theme of this unusual toy railroad coach that carries political banners and signs reading "I Like Ike" and "Vote For Ike." The coach has metal wheels and a plastic body, and it lights up from the inside. Made by Lionel, the Eisenhower Presidential Campaign Car is 12½" long and represents an excellent modern-day 3-D item. **$90**

Comic book portrayals of the candidates helped win support for Dwight Eisenhower and Adlai Stevenson in 1952—and Eisenhower went on to win the election. A campaign kepi with Ike's smiling likeness was worn by many of his backers to help remind voters of his excellent war record. Each comic book **$10**; Ike kepi **$30**

Presidential tiles have been collectible since the last century. This one, using a familiar theme, shows the Eisenhowers. The size is 6" × 6". **$12**

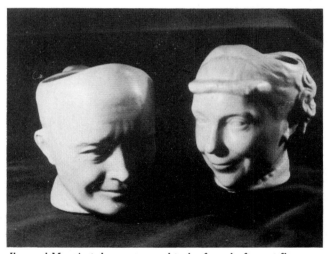

Ike and Mamie toby mugs used to be found often at flea markets, but in recent years they have all but disappeared. They make an excellent addition to any presidential collection since they exude a "first family" image much more dramatically than the more common souvenir plates. The President Eisenhower toby is 5" high, while Mamie is 4½". Each **$25**

The little schoolhouse in Ripon, Wisconsin, where the Republican Party is said to have been born in 1854 is honored by this plate produced in 1954 when Dwight Eisenhower was president. Abraham Lincoln was the first elected republican president, so he is pictured on the party Centennial plate with Eisenhower. Information about the schoolhouse is given on the reverse side. The plate, with a diameter of 9¼", was made by the Homer Laughlin firm. **$15**

For those Americans who like to say "I'll drink to that," there was a whiskey bottle made to commemorate the inauguration of Dwight Eisenhower in 1953. The front of the bottle pictures the Capitol, and the back lists the names of the presidents, their birthdates, home states, and years of inauguration. A worthwhile memento, it stands 11¼" high. **$20**

Americans liked Ike and liked Mamie, and that's why the plate picturing them under the heading "America's First Family" was popular with buyers when the Eisenhowers were in the White House. The transfer is in full color, and the plate, which has a 9" diameter, has a gold trim on the border. **$18**

A metal bank made in the image of President Eisenhower still turns up with frequency in antiques shops and at flea markets. The bank is 5" high. **$15**

All the presidents through Dwight Eisenhower are pictured on this china plate, which sold in souvenir shops during Eisenhower's two terms. Diameter, 7¼". $12

Smokers were not ignored in the campaign to get Dwight Eisenhower elected president. This brightly packaged and still-unopened pack of cigarettes pictures a smiling Ike along with his well-remembered slogan. The campaign packs were produced by the Tobacco Blending Corporation of Louisville, Kentucky. $15

1952 Presidential Election

$8 $8 $8 $9 $10

$8 $9 $30 $8 $9

$7 $8 $4 $3 $15

$9 $7 $6 $3.50

$7 $8 $8 $12

WE NEED ADLAI BADLY
$10

REPUBLICANS FOR STEVENSON
$7

$5 I AM A STEVENSON TEAM MEMBER
$10

$5 I AM A STEVENSON CAPTAIN
$12

STEVENSON
$2

STEVENSON
$2

STEVENSON AND SPARKMAN
$3

UNDERWOOD STEVENSON SPARKMAN
$12

VOTE STEVENSON
$3

ALL THE WAY WITH ADLAI
$6

LABOR FOR STEVENSON
$10

OUR NEXT PRESIDENT ADLAI STEVENSON
$5

FOR PRESIDENT ADLAI E. STEVENSON
$30

FOR PRESIDENT ADLAI E STEVENSON
$7

ADLAI E. STEVENSON
$6

ADLAI E. STEVENSON
$18

I LIKE STEVENSON
$10

GO FORWARD WITH STEVENSON SPARKMAN
$20

OUR NEXT PRESIDENT ADLAI STEVENSON
DEMOCRATIC NATIONAL CONVENTION —1952— CHICAGO
CONVENTION BUILDING INTERNATIONAL AMPHITHEATRE
$15

FORWARD WITH STEVENSON
$8

$5

$8

$10 $10

$45 $40

1956 Presidential Election

$4 $7 $10

$30 $7 $6 $7

$6 $15 $8 $6 $5

$4 $7 $8 $2 $3

$3 $3 $2 $2 $3

$3 $3 $3 $5 $5

$20

$6 $4 $5 $3 $5 $3 $3

$3 $10 $3 $5 $25 $6

$25 $8 $25 $35 $15

$20 $15 $25

$350 $325 $35

$240

Don't let this happen to YOU!

VOTE FOR IKE!

$10

DEMOCRATS FOR DWIGHT D. EISENHOWER

$17

FOR PRESIDENT ADLAI E. STEVENSON

$15

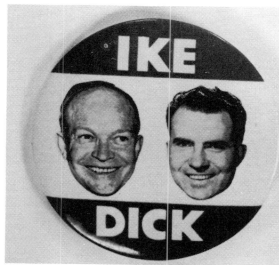

IKE DICK

$12

$40

President John F. Kennedy and Mrs. Kennedy are pictured on this little souvenir china creamer marketed in Washington, D.C. gift shops. It stands 3¾" high. **$10**

John F. Kennedy's smiling face is used on this clear glass tumbler to express the political sentiments of the "Van Buren County Democrats." Height, 4½". **$15**

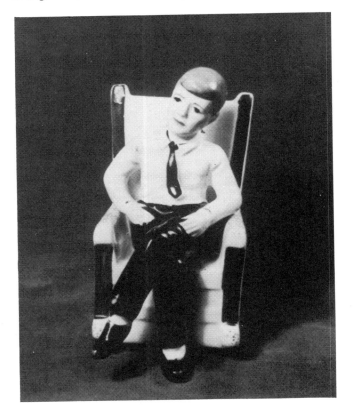

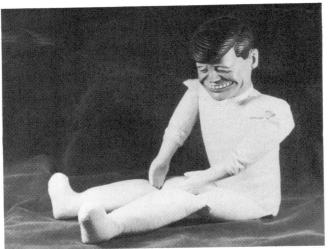

A smiling John F. Kennedy doll which stands more than 20" tall is a favorite with many collectors who specialize in JFK items. The doll has a composition head; the body, except for the hands, is cloth. The Kennedy doll looks great in a tuxedo. **$100**

An amusing presidential collectible, this Japanese-made salt and pepper set is designed to represent John F. Kennedy sitting in his famous rocker. The holes for pouring the salt are in Kennedy's back, while the pepper holes are on the back on the rocker. It's an interesting souvenir. **$28**

Another of the many souvenir china dishes that were made when President John F. Kennedy and his wife, Jackie, brought youth and beauty to the White House, this heart-shaped dish—with the Kennedys pictured in color—was made in Japan. The width is 5". **$12**

A memorial tumbler shows the enameled bust of John F. Kennedy, the dates of his birth and death, and quotations from his famous 1961 inaugural address. **$15**

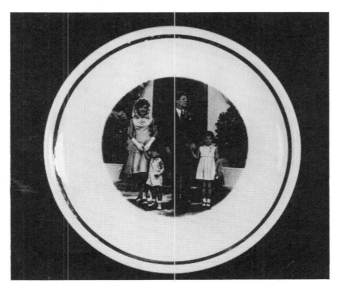

Many Americans recall the Camelot days of the John F. Kennedy presidency in a family scene such as this one. The president and his wife, Jackie, are shown in color with Caroline and little John-John. Diameter, 9". **$20**

Party members were riding the coattails of President John F. Kennedy when the democrats of Indiana held their state convention in 1962. That's why Kennedy's profile appears on this convention badge that also boosts Matt Welsh. **$15**

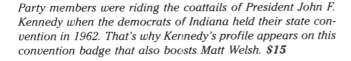

Personality bottle tops were made in the shape of the United States presidents. This one, showing John F. Kennedy, is still in the original box. It was made in Japan and stands 5" high. **$20**

John F. Kennedy and Jackie salt and pepper shakers sell well to presidential collectors. Here are two types. The more common round shakers are shown at the top; the flat-sided monument-type shakers are pictured on the bottom. The round shakers are 2¾" high; the others are 2" tall. Round, pair **$6**; Flat, pair **$10**

Those who collect the presidential plates will like this one featuring John F. Kennedy. Although the likenesses of some of the presidents may be faulted, the color is good and the plate is attractive. Diameter, 10⅛". **$20**

Inexpensive mourning plates were turned out in abundance after the assassination of President John F. Kennedy. The one shown at the top has a diameter of 7". The diameter of the other is 8". Each **$9**

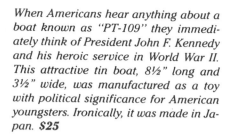

When Americans hear anything about a boat known as "PT-109" they immediately think of President John F. Kennedy and his heroic service in World War II. This attractive tin boat, 8½" long and 3½" wide, was manufactured as a toy with political significance for American youngsters. Ironically, it was made in Japan. **$25**

Delegates to the 1960 Democratic National convention had fun wearing these "straw" hats in support of their favorite candidate, John Kennedy. **$15**

John F. Kennedy is portrayed in this modern, metal-ringed glass paperweight, one of a series. Good likeness of Kennedy in bas-relief. Diameter, 3". **$28**

The assassinated Kennedy brothers, John and Robert, are shown on this color plate, a worthy addition to any presidential collection. John Kennedy was slain while in the White House. Robert was gunned down while campaigning for the presidency. Their deaths are a tragic reminder of the violence that too frequently befalls the nation's leaders. Diameter, 7". **$20**

The serving trays that recall the Kennedy years in the White House were made as a memorial to the assassinated president. The trays, each with an 8¼" diameter, feature the full-color pictures of John F. Kennedy and his wife, Jacqueline, on cardboard. Pair *$30*

Sets of tumblers were sold as a memorial to the assassinated Jonn F. Kennedy. This one pictures Kennedy in blue, framed by a wreath, with the dates 1917–1963. The back is decorated with PT-Boat 109, Kennedy's rocking chair, his "Ask Not What Your Country Can Do for You . . ." quotation, and the eternal flame. A thoughtful piece, it's appropriate for any presidential collection. Height, 5½". *$15*

1960 Presidential Election

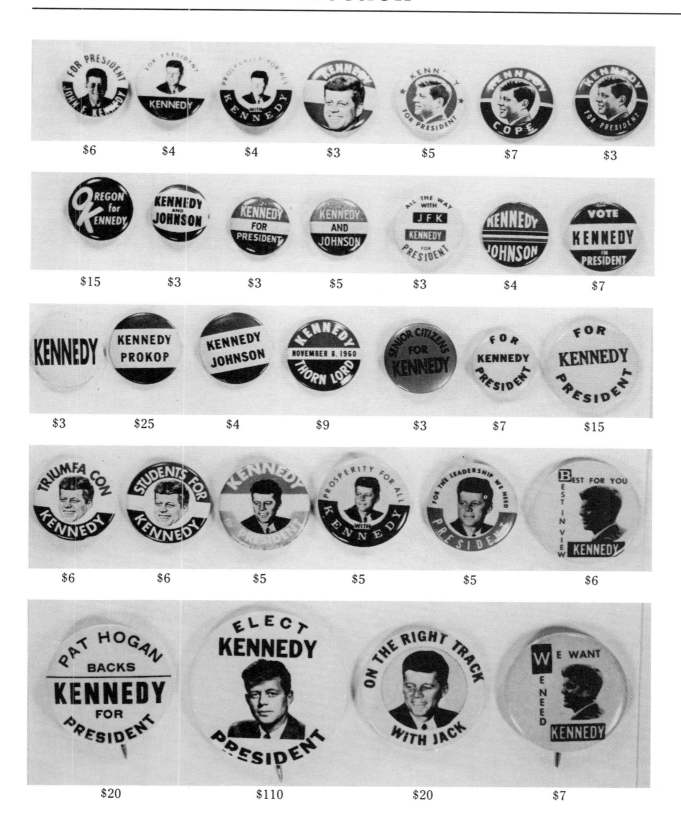

$6 $4 $4 $3 $5 $7 $3

$15 $3 $3 $5 $3 $4 $7

$3 $25 $4 $9 $3 $7 $15

$6 $6 $5 $5 $5 $6

$20 $110 $20 $7

$7	$5	$2	$4	$3	$2	$5
$3	$4	$4	$4	$5	$4	$4
$10	$3	$2	$2	$4	$2	$2
$5	$3	$3	$4	$4	$3	$3
$3	$5	$5	$3	$3	$5	$3

$7	$5	$5	$5	$5

$8 $6 $15 $7

FOR PRESIDENT
JOHN F. KENNEDY

America Needs
KENNEDY–JOHNSON

PROGRESS FOR ALL
FORWARD WITH
KENNEDY

FOR PRESIDENT
RICHARD M. NIXON

LEADERS OF OUR COUNTRY
KENNEDY & JOHNSON
AND A FRIENDLY WORLD

MAN OF STEEL
RICHARD NIXON

$17 $45

$6

Pat FOR
FIRST LADY

EXPERIENCE COUNTS
VOTE
NIXON   LODGE
FOR PRESIDENT   FOR VICE PRESIDENT
FOR
A BETTER AMERICA

$6 $15

A WINNING TEAM
Pat & Dick Nixon

$10

Lyndon B. Johnson
1963–1969

The initials "LBJ" and the cowboy hat tell the presidential collector that this is a bumper sticker made for Lyndon Baines Johnson, our 36th president. The size is 7¼" long × 3⅝" wide; the colors are yellow and black. *$5*

The LBJ style is evident in this 1964 presidential campaign hat, which many democrats wore with pride as Johnson went on to an overwhelming victory over Barry Goldwater. *$12*

An LBJ belt buckle dramatized the lifestyle of President Lyndon Johnson, who enjoyed entertaining friends at the LBJ Ranch in Texas. Size, 2" × 3¼". *$10*

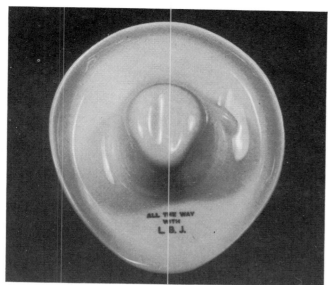

An ashtray in the shape of LBJ's hat makes an interesting and relatively inexpensive souvenir. The hat is 6" long and 5" wide. **$18**

When Nelson Rockefeller made a strong presidential bid in 1964, this umbrella was one of his campaign items. The umbrella is brightly colored, and Rockefeller's picture is shown in the panels. It bears the slogan "Rockefeller for President." Height, 30". **$55**

With "Super LBJ" on the cover, here's a comic book giving an imaginative portrayal of the presidency. As it says on the back cover, it's a case of "guns, butter and laughs." An amusing addition for any presidential collector. Dimensions, 10" × 7". **$15**

Lyndon B. Johnson is the subject of this presidential bottle-top still in its original box. We're not sure whether the Japanese designer really captured the LBJ look, but it's now a collectible. Height, 5". **$15**

Presidents up to and including Lyndon Johnson are pictured on items that were made as souvenirs during the years that LBJ was in the White House. This teapot, which shows the presidential images in color, is 5¼" high. It was imported in 1966 by the Chadwick-Miller firm, as the backstamp indicates. **$18**

The "Win with Barry" slogan on the box of this 1964 dashboard doll of Senator Barry Goldwater didn't get him elected, but it helped preserve his image. A similar dashboard doll was made for Lyndon Johnson. The boxes of these dolls also were attractively decorated by Remco Industries, Incorporated, Harrison, New Jersey. The boxed doll is 7¼" high, 5¼" wide. **$15**

Some good-looking mementos honoring the president were made while Lyndon Johnson was in office. Among them is this well-executed bust of Johnson, produced in 1966. It carries the copyright name of Jimilu Mason on the side, along with the year. The Johnson bust is 9" high. **$30**

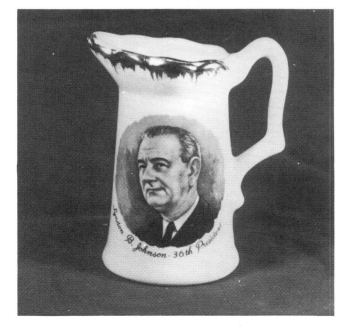

President Johnson was pictured on many souvenirs sold in Washington, D.C. shops during his years in the White House. This little full-color pitcher is an example of the type of item available at the time, 3¾" high. **$12**

A happy family image is projected from this ceramic cup picturing President Lyndon Johnson, his wife Lady Bird, and daughters Lynda Bird and Luci Baines. Height, 3¼". **$8**

A tin serving tray with a cardboard color picture of President Johnson is among the collectibles that still can be easily found. The same kind of plate-size tray was made for John F. Kennedy. **$12**

Barry Goldwater made a run for the presidency in 1964, and this gold-trimmed tumbler was one of his campaign items. It pictures a smiling Goldwater, lists the year (1964), and shows an elephant behind the familiar H_2O symbol. Well-made, the tumbler stands 5½" high. **$15**

A presidential plate showing the former chief executives in brown transfer prints was made with Lyndon Johnson in the center. Green leaves decorate the center circle and border. An interesting plate, larger than most, with a diameter of 10¼". **$18**

President Lyndon Johnson and his wife, Lady Bird, are captured in a rather formal pose on this souvenir china plate. The transfer print is in the customary color on this plate, which has a diameter of 9". **$15**

Both LBJ and Lady Bird are pictured on this cup and saucer combination made as a souvenir while Lyndon Johnson was in the White House. The cup is 2¾" high, and the plate has a diameter of 6". $15

$1.50	$1.50	$1.50	$2.25	$1.75	$3	$1.50	$1.25
$1	$2	$1	$2	$2	$2.50	$2.50	$3
$4	$3	$4	$5	$3.50	$2	$4	
$3	$12	$2	$5	$6	$4		
$3.50	$3	$5	$5	$4			
$9	$4	$5	$3				

$2 $2.50 $2 $3 $2 $2 $2 $2

$6 $4 $3 $2 $4 $4 $4

$4 $15 $10 $5 $4 $4

$2.50 $3 $3 $3 $4 $5 $7

$4 $3 $4.50 $4.50 $5 $5

$3 $4 $3 $3 $5

$6

$5

$7

$25

$7

$5

$6

DEMOCRATS ARE WE FOR JOHNSON & HUMPHREY

$5

$2

$2

$5

$3

$4

Richard M. Nixon
1969–1974

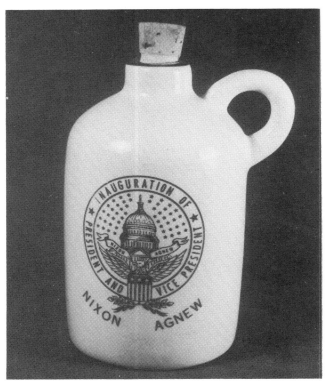

A corked jug was made as an inauguration souvenir for Richard Nixon and Spiro Agnew. The 4¾" jugs carry the Nixon and Agnew names and a picture of the Capitol dome. **$18**

Spiro Agnew's troubled days as vice president are recalled by this toy pipe. The bowl is ceramic, and the colored balls on the stem are made of wood. A good item for those who appreciate the historic significance of the disintegration of the presidency of Richard Nixon. From end to end, the little pipe measures 4¼". **$40**

Hubert H. Humphrey and Edmund Muskie are embossed on the sides of this rich green glass figural campaign bottle made in 1968 by the Wheaton Company in Millville, New Jersey. The medallion images of the candidates also bear the 1968 date. Good items, they're still often underpriced on today's market. Height, 7". **$15**

Autographed by Richard Nixon and his wife, Pat, this 1968 Lincoln Day dinner ticket is framed against a newspaper artist's sketch of a school gymnasium that provided a typical setting for many campaign speeches that year. In November of 1968, Nixon was elected president. **$175**

This 1968 campaign bank championed the cause of Richard Nixon and Spiro Agnew. On one side is embossed "Nixon 68 Agnew." The other is marked "GOP." A good little remembrance of that election, especially when coupled with the companion democratic donkey bank. Iron, and just 2¾" high. **$45**

When Hubert Humphrey and Edmund Muskie teamed up to op-
pose Richard Nixon and Spiro Agnew in the 1968 presidential
contest, these little iron donkey banks appeared as campaign
items. They have been moving steadily into the hands of collectors, but some still can be found. One side reads, "Humphrey Muskie 68" and the other carries the word, "Democrat."
Height, 4¼". *$45*

Pre-Watergate days in the White House were satisfying ones
for President Richard Nixon and his wife, Pat. Their smiling
image is shown in color on a typical souvenir china plate with
a diameter of 9". *$15*

Dressed in a red, white, and blue outfit and wearing a banner
that reads, "Nixon for president," the 6" elephant shown here
is a head nodder. The head wiggles whichever way it is di-
rected to wiggle by way of a spring. There's also a spring in the
elephant's trunk. A clever campaign novelty. *$25*

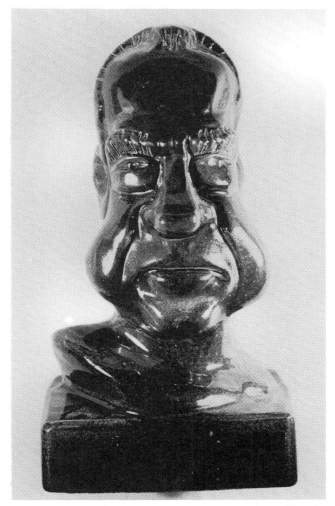

Richard Nixon is shown in a ceramic caricature bank. The slot
for money is on the top of Nixon's head. Height, 8¼". *$20*

Americans who had hoped that Robert F. Kennedy could win the nomination of the democratic party and then go on to become president as did his brother, John F. Kennedy, were saddened in 1968. At a time when his campaign seemed to be gaining momentum, Bobby Kennedy was shot and killed in California. Mourning buttons such as the one shown here were worn by many who had supported him. The button has a diameter of 1¾". **$8**

This Nixon toothpick holder was made as a Bicentennial piece—but President Nixon had been driven from office as a result of the Watergate scandal before the national celebration ever began. It's an attractive presidential souvenir nevertheless, showing the bas-relief image of Nixon with George Washington and an American Indian pictured elsewhere around the sides. Stars also appear at the top edge and near the pedestal base. The bottom of this amethyst piece, which is 2½" high, is marked "Original Bob St. Clair, 1776–1976." **$22**

Spiro Agnew watches definitely have become collectible, especially after the shameful manner in which he and President Nixon both were forced to leave office. The watch is about 1½" long. **$55**

Voters were urged to "Click with Dick" in this little Richard Nixon campaign giveaway. Other shapes of clickers also were used. Blue and white, 2½" long. **$8**

The only presidential tandem in history individually pressured to resign was boosted on this campaign jewelry made for Richard Nixon and Spiro Agnew. That alone should make it collectible. The pin is 1¾" high. **$8**

Made to be worn over a clothing button, this attractive red-and-black ribbon was produced for Richard Nixon in his losing 1960 race against John Kennedy. It is a well-made woven ribbon that exceeds in quality most ribbons turned out in recent decades. It is 6" long and 1⅜" wide. **$22**

The Bobby Kennedy presidential boom was brief, but it lasted long enough for these red, white, and blue mugs to be made for his 1968 campaign. He was assassinated in California just when his effort to win the presidency seemed to be picking up support. The mug is 4" high. **$10**

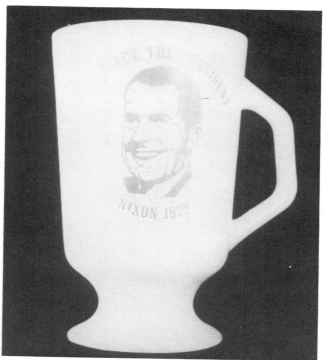

The smiling face of Richard Nixon appears on this white campaign coffee mug made by the Anchor Hocking firm in 1972. Nobody knew it then, but the slogan "Re-elect the President" would later take on a different meaning as the result of the Watergate scandal. Height, 5". **$20**

All the shenanigans associated with the Watergate scandal are recalled in this amusing card game appropriately named "The Watergate Scandal." Some day, collectors will explain to their grandchildren what Watergate was all about—and the cards will provide helpful graphics. **$8**

Jugate ribbons showing the candidates in the memorable 1968 presidential election today have become collectibles. George Wallace and his running mate, Curtis LeMay, advocated the "Stand up for America" theme while Hubert Humphrey and Edmund Muskie carried the democratic party banner in a call for "Unity and Progress." The Wallace ribbon, printed black on yellow, is 6⅞" long, while the orange Humphrey ribbon is 6" long. Wallace **$12**; Humphrey **$15**

Both the figural bottles and the red, white, and blue boxes are eye-catching and well done in the case of the Wheaton Company Nuline campaign items produced in 1968. This photo shows the GOP elephant, with Richard Nixon embossed on one side and Spiro Agnew, the vice presidential nominee, on the other. The base is marked "Republican Campaign." The color is amber, and the bottle stands 7" high. *$15*

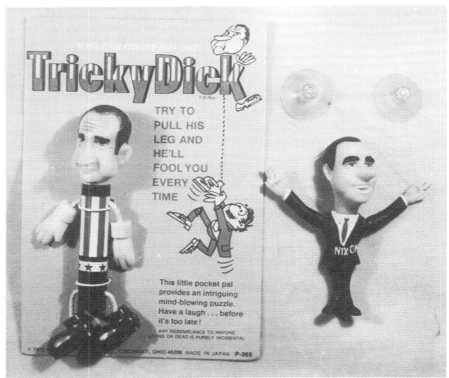

The images that presidents create are always quickly caricatured. On the left we see a "Tricky Dick" novelty designed to "fool you every time." It stands 5" high. On the right a little rubbery Nixon is shown smiling and giving the victory sign. It's 4" tall and is made to dangle from your car or house window. Tricky, on card *$12*; Smiling *$6*

Spiro Agnew is remembered by this pinkish, 4½" glass mug embellished with the GOP symbol in the form of an elephant handle. Embossed on the bottom is "Spiro Agnew, 1970." The mug also carries the marking of the Imperial Glass Company. It's a good reminder of Agnew's troubled days as Nixon's vice president. **$20**

Richard Nixon is centered in a plate that was made for the souvenir shops during his troubled presidency. Portraits of all the presidents are in color, and the 9" plate has a gold border edging. **$18**

1968 Presidential Election

$3 $2 $1.50 $1 $1 $3

$2 $2 $2.50 $5 $3

$2 $1 $1 $1 $1 $1

$4 $2 $2 $4

$3 $6 $2 $1 $1 $1

$3 $4 $6

$2 $1 $2 $1 $1 $1

$4 $3 $3

$3

$12 $2.50 $2.50

$4.50 $3.50

$4

| $3 | $1 | $2 | $2 | $1 |

| $2 | $2 | $2.50 | $2 | $3 |

| $3 | $2.50 | $2.50 | $1.75 | $2 |

| $2 | $3 | $4 | $3 | $7 |

| $3 | $2 | $1 | $3 | $3 | $4 |

1972 Presidential Election

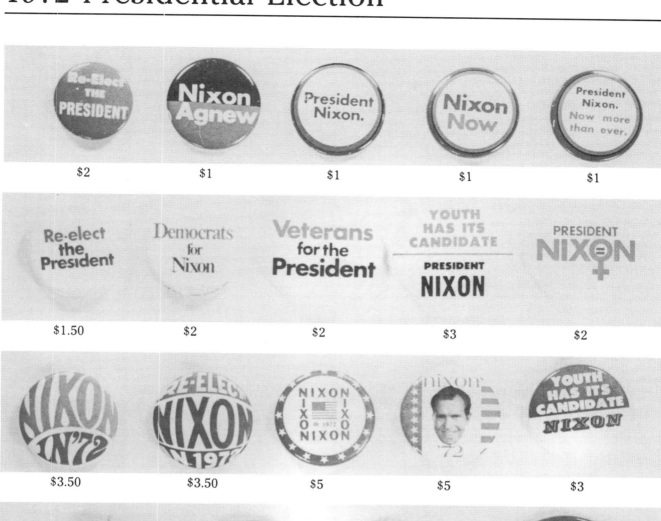

$2	$1	$1	$1	$1
$1.50	$2	$2	$3	$2
$3.50	$3.50	$5	$5	$3

$3	$3	$5	$2.50

$3	$2	$3.50

$2

$2

$2.50

$1.50

$2

$3

$1

$1.50

$5

$5

$2

$2.50

$2

$1

$3

$5

$3

$5

$3

$2

$2

$4 $4

EMK IN 1972

NOTRE DAME STUDENTS for KENNEDY 1972

TED FOR V.P.

PEABODY VICE PRESIDENT

STANLEY ARNOLD VICE PRESIDENT

$2 $5 $5 $2 $2

KENNEDY 72

HUGHES 72

HARTKE FOR PRESIDENT

HOOKED ON MUSKIE

I'm Bayh PARTISAN '72

COLL FOR PRESIDENT

$2 $3 $3 $4 $3 $5

Lindsay

NEW HAMPSHIRE NEEDS YORTY FOR PRESIDENT

HUMPHREY The People's Democrat.

McCarthy March 21

Patsy MINK PRESIDENT

$2 $3 $1 $3 $4

WALLACE FOR PRESIDENT

Common Sense JACKSON FOR PRESIDENT For A Change

ELECT Mills PRESIDENT

Sanford for President

Catalyst for change CHISHOLM for PRESIDENT '72

$1 $1 $3 $2 $3

229

Gerald Ford
1974–1977

His time in office was short, so collectibles from the presidency of Gerald Ford are not around in abundance. This little gift-shop mug identifies him as the 38th president and lists his August 9, 1974, inauguration date. Height, 3¾". $25

Gerald Ford's presidency began with the resignation of Richard Nixon on August 9, 1974, rather than as the result of a campaign that would have produced the usual assortment of collectibles, such as buttons, flags, plates, and so on. Not until the 1976 election were presidential campaign mementos turned out for Ford as he sought the support of voters. But they turned instead to Carter, and that's why such items as this brown-glazed mug, which matches one made for Carter, are eagerly sought by collectors. The Ford mug, incidentally, is harder to find than the Carter version. Height, 4". $40

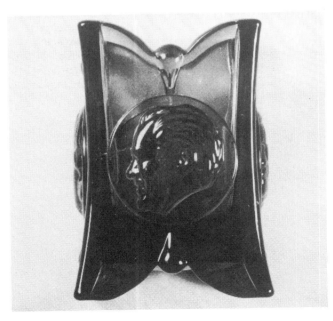

A smiling President Gerald Ford and Mrs. Ford are portrayed in a color transfer in the center of this Washington, D.C. souvenir plate. The plate, with a 9¼" diameter, has gold edging. Items from the Ford presidency will be hard to find in the future. $20

Gerald Ford was in the White House in 1976, the year the nation celebrated its Bicentennial. Made by glassmaker Joe St. Clair, this reddish toothpick holder carries the embossed image of President Ford as well as George Washington and the Liberty Bell. Height, 3". $20

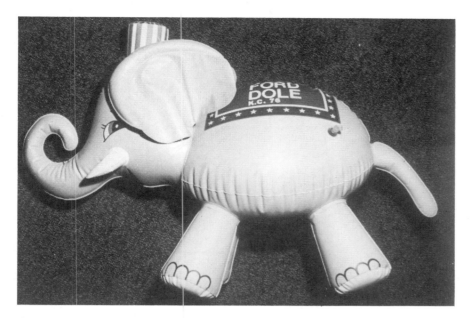

An air-filled, plastic GOP elephant sang the praises of the Ford-Dole team in 1976. This campaign collectible is about 14" high. **$20**

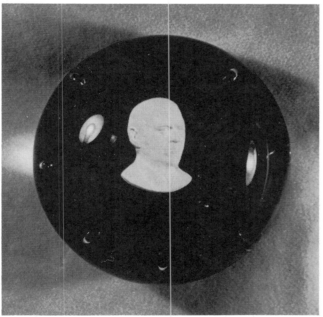

Dated 1975, this domed sulphide paperweight shows President Gerald Ford against a deep blue background. Scarce, it's an excellent souvenir from Ford's limited days in the White House. The bottom is signed "Maude and Bob St. Clair, 1975." Diameter: 3". **$90**

Souvenir platemakers also produced a presidential plate for Gerald Ford. Shown in the center, he is surrounded in the usual manner by all his predecessors. The historic value of these modestly priced plates is enhanced because most of them carry not only portraits of the presidents but the years they served. Diameter, 10". **$20**

Jimmy Carter
1977–1981

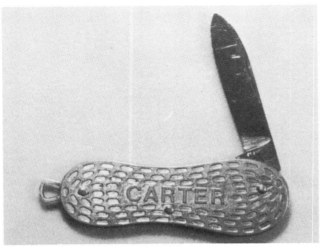

The peanut in all forms was glorified during the Bicentennial-year campaign of Jimmy Carter. Here's a little peanut-shaped, one-bladed jackknife made by Taylor Cutlery, Kingsport, Tennessee. One side of the peanut has the name "Carter," and the other says "Mr. Peanut, Nov.2, 1976." A good campaign memento, 3" long (with the blade closed). *$25*

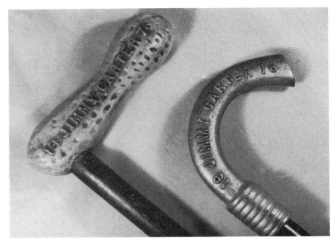

The handles of two canes made for Jimmy Carter's successful bid for the presidency in 1976 reflect the respectable quality of these recent campaign collecibles. One stresses the background of the candidate as a Georgia peanut farmer, and the other is similar to a cane made for the 1932 campaign of Franklin Roosevelt. Peanut handle *$50*; Round handle *$40*

Coffee mugs picturing the presidents have been popular in recent years. This one shows Jimmy Carter with the transfer in color and identifies him as our 39th president. Height, 3⅝". *$18*

A grinning peanut mug was made as a souvenir of Jimmy Carter's years as the country's leader. The peanut handle, the Carter smile, and the boots are all reminders of his presidency. Height, 5¼". *$8*

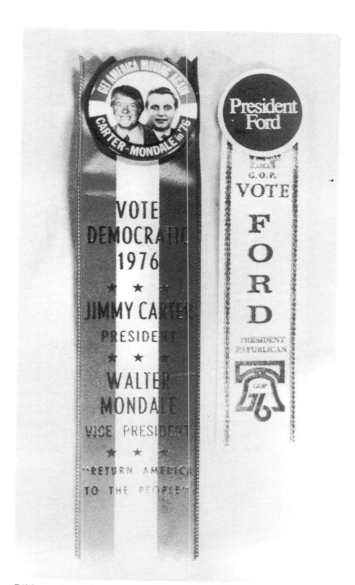

The adaptability of the presidential plate manufacturers is shown in this plate, which was made in Japan. At the center top is Gerald Ford—with his White House departure date stil not listed. To make the plate current after the election, Carter's picture was pasted on above the American eagle. $12

Ribbons from the campaign of 1976, the nation's Bicentennial year, include the Carter-Mondale item in red, white, and blue on the left and the blue-and-white Ford ribbon on the right. Each was pinned to the lapel of campaign backers by the attached buttons. The Carter ribbon is 8¾" long, and the Ford ribbon is 6". Each $10

The shadowed features of President Jimmy Carter are portrayed on this souvenir plate. The president is pictured in color. Diameter, 10¼". $15

Made in Italy, this clear glass, standup paperweight is of good quality and shows the frosted intaglio image of Carter. It was produced around the time of Carter's inauguration. $35

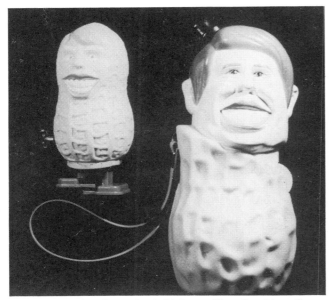

When he ran for the nation's highest office, President Carter was forever reminded that he came from the peanut business. Shown on the left is a collectible 4½" high windup peanut made to look like Carter. It was made in Japan. On the right is a Carter peanut radio, also made of plastic and standing about 7½" high; it was manufactured in Hong Kong. They look gaudy now, but have long-range merit as presidential collectibles. Each **$20**

A peanut holder (or planter) was made after Jimmy Carter had been elected to the presidency. The name "Mel Tiess" is stamped on the back of this humorous collectible. Marketed in plaster shops, the peanut holders also have moved onto the tables at flea markets and shops emphasizing collectibles. Height, 8¾". Painted **$25**

This brown-glazed mug showing the smiling countenance of Jimmy Carter is a fine collectible from the 1976 campaign, when Carter was elected. A matching mug was made for Gerald Ford. Height, 4". **$35**

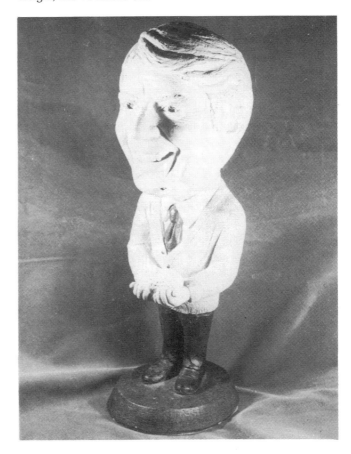

Smiling President Carter, wearing his tan cardigan sweater, is portrayed here as a 16½" plaster statue, apparently offering a peanut to the nation. Fine coloring and good flesh tones on the face make this an interesting collectible. It was made by Esco Products in 1977 and is sure to rise in value. **$55**

This sampling of Jimmy Carter souvenirs shows a deck of "Politicards," a Carter-Mondale jackknife, and a plastic Carter drinking cup. The mug stands 4" high. Cards $6; Jackknife $5; Mug $4

This toothy likeness of Jimmy Carter asking the familiar question, "Jimmy Who?," makes the tumbler a good collectible. The question was asked often when Carter began the campaign that in 1976 took him to the White House. Height, 5½". $8

One of the hits at the 1980 Democratic convention was this cleverly made "Teddy" Kennedy bear. Those who supported the presidential bid of Senator Edward Kennedy had great fun with these bears, almost as much fun, in fact, as do the political collectors. A tag on the side of the "Teddy" bear, manufactured in Los Angeles, reads, "Teddy Bear, 1980, A Unique Collectible, Wes Soderstrom, Woodland Hills, Calif., P. O. Box 60 91365." About 17" high. $50

The Carter-Mondale campaign team is pictured on this pocket watch shown with a Carter watch fob. The watches, particularly, should increase in value in the years ahead. Watch $42; Fob $8

1976 Presidential Election

$1 $1 $1.50 $2 $1.50 $1

$2 $1 $2 $2 $2

$2 $2.50 $3 $3 $1.50

$1.50 $3 $4 $2

$2.50 $1.50 $2 $2.50

$1.50	$2	$5	$5	$1

$4	$1.50	$1.50	$1.50	$1.50

$1.50	$2	$1.50	$2	$2

$2	$2	$2	$3

$3	$2	$2.50	$2

$1 $1 $1 $1 $2 $1

$2 $2 $1 $2

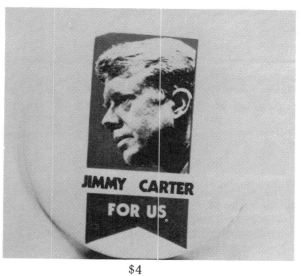

$4

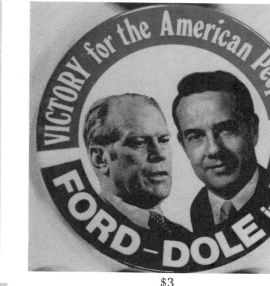

$3

$4

$7

Ronald Reagan
1981

President Ronald Reagan and Vice President George Bush are pictured on this star-trimmed, gold-edged, flag-waving plate made to observe Reagan's inauguration. An attractive souvenir bearing the inaugural seal, the 10¼" plate was made in a limited edition on fine porcelain china by Wildlife Art, Ltd. of California. The art is from a painting by Douglas VanHowd. **$65**

Made for the Republican National Convention in Kansas City in 1976, this Ronald Reagan glass has joined the list of collectibles. Reagan's image and the printing are frosted on clear glass. It is 3¼" high. **$10**

How about a paperweight that captures forever an actual piece of the oak platform on which Ronald Reagan and other dignitaries stood when he was inaugurated on January 20, 1981? Hall-Schuman & Associates of Verona, Pennsylvania, offered such an authenticated souvenir, with a 3" × 1" piece of the flooring, plus a copper inaugural medal encased in Lucite. It seems likely that these will increse in value over the years. The original price was just $28 plus shipping. Attractive, 6¼" long and 3" high. **$40**

The "First Family" paper doll and cutout book showing President and Mrs. Reagan on the cover has been popular with collectors everywhere. It is 9" × 12" and provides some delightful outfits plus decorations for the Oval Office. Published by Dell Publishing Company, 1 Dag Hammarskjold Plaza, New York, New York. **$8**

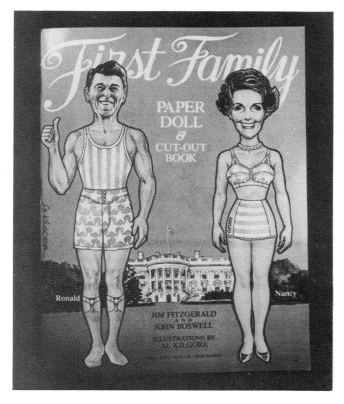

Two postcards, one showing President Reagan and Mrs. Reagan in a parody of a long-familiar painting, and the other picturing President Reagan and his vice president, George Bush, have been widely circulated. Also shown is a Reagan-Bush jackknife. These items, along with a wide assortment of buttons, are among the current collectibles. Reagan-Mrs. Reagan **$1**; Reagan-Bush **$1**; Knife **$5**

This little two-party bank is certain to become a desired collectible from the 1984 election. On one side, it carries the embossed names "Reagan Bush, 84," and on the other can be found "Mondale Ferraro, 84." The head of a smiling elephant peers from one end and a happy donkey looks out from the other. The money slots are on the top. The bank is painted gray and is trimmed in gold. Collectors have a special fondness for the bank because of Geraldine Ferraro's place on the democratic ticket. The bank is 3¼" high and 6" wide. Made by Reynolds Toys of Falls Church, Virginia. **$90**

Salt and pepper shakers have been standard souvenirs of our American presidents for the last few decades—and Ronald Reagan is no exception. The president's image is in color. Height, 3". Pair **$5**

A Frankoma elephant carries a 1981 date and the names of Reagan and Bush. The other side of the elephant has the familiar "GOP." Height, 4". **$15**

Mechanical banks that have appeared during the presidency of Ronald Reagan include the one on the left, which stands 9" high. It is known as the "Reaganomics" bank and shows a poor likeness of the president wearing a cowboy hat and ready to deposit coins in a satchel marked "Jelly Beans," similar to the old Uncle Sam banks. The bank on the right shows the president addressing members of Congress in front of a gavel-wielding Tip O'Neill. When money is placed in the slot above Reagan's head, O'Neill pounds it into the bank with his gavel. The Reaganomics bank is dated 1983 by A-America, Incorporated, and the "Great Political Feud" bank with O'Neill and Reagan was made in 1983 by Miley's Incorporated of Marion, Ohio. The O'Neill bank is 9½" high. Reaganomics **$30**; Reagan-O'Neill **$35**

Jugate bottles made for the delegates to the national party conventions in 1984 rank among the good glass presidential collectibles of the last two decades. On the left is the democratic bottle, showing the embossed likenesses of Walter Mondale and Geraldine Ferraro. The bottle on the right pictures President Reagan and George Bush. The neck of each bottle is decorated with stars, and the reverse sides carry the elephant and donkey symbols, list the site and dates for the convention, and also have an indented area for the paste-in of the delegate's name. Made in dark and light amber by Clevenger Brothers Glassworks, Clayton, New Jersey. Height, 7½". Each **$30**

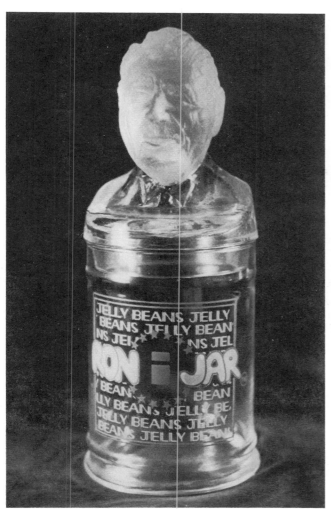

Reagan's second inauguration on Jan. 20, 1985 is featured on this heavy tumbler which carries the frosted images of the president as well as vice president George Bush. It is 4⅛" high. $12

An item that seems destined to survive as a desired souvenir of Ronald Reagan's years in the White House is this glass "Ron Jar"—for holding jellybeans. Standing 10¾" high, with a diameter of 3⅞", the unusual jar features a heavy lid that could easily serve as a paperweight. Reagan's head is frosted, and it's a reasonably good likeness of the president. The base is much more fragile than the heavy 5¾" lid, however, and many may not endure if used regularly. It's an interesting souvenir from a president who has given new prominence to the jellybean. $65

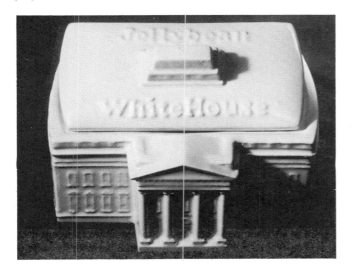

Jellybeans gained national prominence when President Ronald Reagan took office. One of the more interesting collectibles with that tasty theme is a ceramic "Jellybean White House." The top lifts off and inside, of course, are jellybeans. A label on the base of the 5½" × 4⅝" souvenir shows that it was distributed by Ego Enterprises of Barrington, Illinois. Because the knob is a little slippery to grasp, the all-important tops may suffer breakage over the years. Those that survive intact will beome more desirable when the Reagan years fade into history. $28

1980 Presidential Election

$3 $.75 $.50 $.75 $.75

$2 $2 $2 $2 $4

$2 $3 $2 $2

$.75 $1 $1 $.75 $.75

$3 $3 $4

$3 $3 $5

$7 $3

$1 $1 $1.50 $5

$3 $2 $1.50 $2

$1.50 $4 $2 $2.50

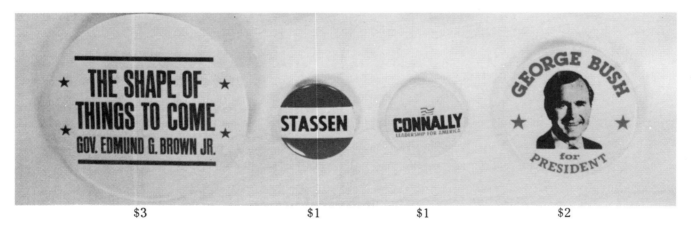

$8 $3

$3 $1 $1 $2

$3 $2.50 $1 $1

Kennedy '80

'80

Kennedy '80

PHIL CRANE FOR PRESIDENT

$.50	$2	$3	$2

1984 Presidential Election

REAGAN '84

REAGAN BUSH

ELECTION NIGHT NOVEMBER 6 1984
REAGAN BUSH '84
WASHINGTON DC

President Reagan '84

American Heroes
REAGAN

$2	$2	$10	$2	$3

DEMOCRATS FOR REAGAN

REAGAN BUSH

WOMEN FOR REAGAN

WOMEN for REAGAN

$2	$3	$2	$2

RE-ELECT THE PRESIDENT

AMERICA NEEDS REAGAN in '84

ILLINOIS LAND OF REAGAN

KEEP AMERICA GREAT
RE-ELECT REAGAN BUSH in '84

$1.50	$3	$5	$1.50

FRITZ IS THE PITZ

REAGAN

REAGAN BUSH '84

REAGAN BUSH '84

REAGAN BUSH '84

$1	$1	$.50	$.50	$.50

$2 $2 $3

MONDALE '84 **MONDALE FERRARO** **MONDALE '84** **MONDALE** **MONDALE FERRARO**

$3 $.50 $2 $.50 $2

Another REPUBLICAN for FERRARO

MONDALE

MONDALE FERRARO 1984

MONDALE FERRARO NOW

$2 $2 $2 $5 $2

AMERICA NEEDS NEW LEADERSHIP 1984 MONDALE-FERRARO

MONDALE FERRARO

AFSCME MONDALE

DEMOCRATIC INTEGRITY — Walter Mondale in '84

$1 $4 $2.50 $3.50

GLASS, POTTERY, PLASTICS & ALLIED WORKERS AFL-CIO CLC — FRITZ MONDALE GERRY FERRARO

MONDALE-FERRARO FOR NEW LEADERSHIP

DEMOCRATIC NATIONAL CONVENTION — SAN FRANCISCO · JULY 16-19 · 1984

$40 $3 $3

PRESIDENT MONDALE UFCW — Mondale Ferraro — FOR MONDALE — AFSCME for MONDALE FERRARO — Nurses for MONDALE/FERRARO

$.75 $2 $2 $1 $7

Take Hart '84 — JESSE JACKSON PRESIDENT '84 — CRANSTON '84 — John Glenn 84 — Askew FOR PRESIDENT

$.75 $.75 $3 $.50 $.50

TO KEEP OUR NATION FIRM
GIVE HIM ANOTHER TERM!
REAGAN '84
YR NATIONAL CONVENTION 1981

$4

GERALDINE FERRARO 1984 1984 AMERICA'S 1st WOMAN VICE PRES.

$2

AMERICA 1984 1984 LOVES REAGAN

$2

$1

MONDALE IN '84

$2

McGovern

$.50

249

Hopefuls in 1988

$1

$5

$2

$2

$2

$1

$2

$1.50

$1

$1.50 $2 $1.50 $1.50

The Presidents and Many of the Also-Rans

Over the years, numerous obscure candidates have sought the office of the presidency. This list makes no claim to include them all, but it shows the names of many who were familiar to a wide audience of the nation's voters.

1789
George Washington, president
John Adams, vice president

Others supported: John Jay, Robert Harrison, John Rutledge, John Hancock, George Clinton, Samuel Huntington, John Milton, James Armstrong, Benjamin Lincoln, Edward Telfair

1792
George Washington, president
John Adams, vice president

Others supported: George Clinton, Thomas Jefferson, Aaron Burr

1796
John Adams, president
Thomas Jefferson, vice president

Others supported: Thomas Pinckney, Aaron Burr, Samuel Adams, Oliver Ellsworth, George Clinton, John Jay, James Iredell, John Henry, Samuel Johnson, George Washington, Charles Pinckney

1800
Thomas Jefferson, president
Aaron Burr, vice president

Others supported: John Adams, Charles Pinckney, John Jay

1804
Thomas Jefferson, president
George Clinton, vice president

Others supported: Charles Pinckney

1808
James Madison, president
George Clinton, vice president

Others supported: Charles Pinckney

1812
James Madison, president
Elbridge Gerry, vice president

Others supported: Dewitt Clinton

1816
James Monroe, president
Daniel Tompkins, vice president

Others supported: Rufus King

1820
James Monroe, president
Daniel Tompkins, vice president

Others supported: John Quincy Adams

1824
John Quincy Adams, president
John Calhoun, vice president

Others supported: Andrew Jackson, William H. Crawford, Henry Clay

1828
Andrew Jackson, president
John C. Calhoun, vice president

Others supported: John Quincy Adams

1832
Andrew Jackson, president
Martin Van Buren, vice president

Others supported: Henry Clay, John Floyd, William Wirt

1836
Martin Van Buren, president
Richard M. Johnson, vice president

Others supported: William H. Harrison, Daniel Webster, Hugh L. White, William P. Mangum

1840
William H. Harrison, president
John Tyler, vice president

Others supported: Martin Van Buren, James G. Birney

Among the rarities in political collecting are the eight shown here. First column: (top) age-faded Washington Benevolent Society ribbon, circa 1815, used as a bookmark, $250; (bottom) silver Jefferson inaugural medal, $14,000. Second column: (top) Van Buren medalet, $350; Lincoln oval ferrotype from 1860 campaign, $1,200; Polk medalet, $450; unusual Douglas clothing button ferrotype, $1,000. Third column: (top) William H. Harrison sulphide, $1500; (bottom) Buchanan campaign ribbon with excellent graphics but which happens to be in poor condition, $200. (In good condition, the 7" Buchanan ribbon would bring $500.)

1844

James K. Polk, president

George M. Dallas, vice president

Others supported: Henry Clay, James G. Birney

1848

Zachary Taylor, president

Millard Fillmore, vice president

Others supported: Lewis Cass, Martin Van Buren

1852

Franklin Pierce, president

William R. King, vice president

Others supported: Winfield Scott, John P. Hale

1856

James Buchanan, president

John C. Breckinridge, vice president

Others supported: John C. Fremont, Millard Fillmore

1860

Abraham Lincoln, president

Hannibal Hamlin, vice president

Others supported: John C. Breckinridge, Stephen Douglas, John Bell, Jefferson Davis

1864

Abraham Lincoln, President

Andrew Johnson, vice president

Others supported: George B. McClellan

1868

Ulysses S. Grant, president

Schuyler Colfax, vice president

Others supported: Horatio Seymour

1872

Ulysses S. Grant, president

Henry Wilson, vice president

Others supported: Horace Greeley, Charles O'Conor, James Black, Thomas Hendricks, Charles J. Jenkins, David Davis, Victoria Woodhull, William Groesbeck

1876

Rutherford B. Hayes, president

William A. Wheeler, vice president

Others supported: Samuel J. Tilden, Peter Cooper, Green C. Smith, James B. Walker

1880

James A. Garfield, president

Chester A. Arthur, vice president

Others supported: Winfield S. Hancock, James B. Weaver, Neal Dow, John W. Phelps

1884

Grover Cleveland, president

Thomas A. Hendricks, vice president

Others supported: James G. Blaine, John P. St. John, Benjamin F. Butler, P. D. Wiggington, Mrs. Belva Lockwood, Samuel C. Pomeroy

1888

Benjamin Harrison, president

Levi P. Morton, vice president

Others supported: Grover Cleveland, Clinton B. Fisk, Alson J. Streeter, R. H. Cowdrey, James L. Curtis, Mrs. Belva Lockwood

1892

Grover Cleveland, president

Adlai E. Stevenson, vice president

Others supported: Benjamin Harrison, James B. Weaver, John Bidwell, Simon Wing

1896

William McKinley, president

Garret A. Hobart, vice president

Others supported: William J. Bryan, John M. Palmer, Joshua Levering, Charles H. Matchett, Charles E. Bentley

1900

William McKinley, president

Theodore Roosevelt, vice president

Others supported: William J. Bryan, John G. Wooley, Eugene Debs, Joseph F. Malloney, Wharton Barker, Donelson Caffery, Seth H. Ellis, Jonah F. Leonard

1904

Theodore Roosevelt, president

Charles W. Fairbanks, vice president

Others supported: Alton B. Parker, Silas C. Swallow, Eugene Debs, Charles H. Corrigan, Thomas E. Watson, George E. Taylor, Austin H. Holcomb

1908

William H. Taft, president

James S. Sherman, vice president

Others supported: William J. Bryan, Eugene W. Chafin, Eugene V. Debs, August Gillhaus, Thomas E. Watson, Thomas L. Hisgen, W. R. Benkert, Daniel B. Turney

1912

Woodrow Wilson, president

Thomas R. Marshall, vice president

Others supported: Theodore Roosevelt, William Howard Taft, Eugene V. Debs, Eugene W. Chafin, Arthur E. Reimer, Blauford F. Ziggfeld

1916
Woodrow Wilson, president
Thomas R. Marshall, vice president

Others supported: Charles Evans Hughes, Alan L. Benson, James F. Hanley, Hollister Purdue, Arthur E. Reimer

1920
Warren G. Harding, president
Calvin Coolidge, vice president

Others supported: James M. Cox, Aaron S. Watkins, Parley P. Christensen, Eugene V. Debs, William W. Cox, Robert C. Macauley, James E. Ferguson

1924
Calvin Coolidge, president
Charles G. Dawes, vice president

Others supported: John W. Davis, Herman P. Faris, William Z. Foster, Frank T. Johns, Robert M. LaFollette, William Wallace, John Zahnd, Gilbert Nations, Jacob S. Coxey, Benson A. Cropp

1928
Herbert Hoover, president
Charles Curtis, vice president

Others supported: Alfred E. Smith, Norman Thomas, William Z. Foster, Verne L. Reynolds, William Varney, Frank Webb, John Zahnd, Wilcox Rondo, Dr. Henry Hoffman

1932
Franklin D. Roosevelt, president
John N. Garner, vice president

Others supported: Herbert Hoover, Norman Thomas, William Z. Foster, William D. Upshaw, William H. Harvey, Verne L. Reynolds, Jacob S. Coxey, John Zahnd, James R. Cox, Laven Keshibian

1936
Franklin D. Roosevelt, president
John N. Garner, vice president

Others supported: Alfred M. Landon, William Lemke, Norman Thomas, Earl Russell Browder, David Leigh Colvin, John W. Aiken, William Pelley, John Zahnd

1940
Franklin D. Roosevelt, president
Henry A. Wallace, vice president

Others supported: Wendell Willkie, Norman Thomas, Roger Ward Babson, Earl Russell Browder, John W. Aiken, Alfred Knutson, John Zahnd, Anna Milburn

1944
Franklin D. Roosevelt, president
Harry S. Truman, vice president

Others supported: Thomas E. Dewey, Norman Thomas, Claude A. Watson, Edward A. Teichert, Gerald L. K. Smith

1948
Harry S. Truman, president
Alben W. Barkley, vice president

Others supported: Thomas E. Dewey, J. Strom Thurmond, Henry A. Wallace, Norman Thomas, Claude A. Watson, Edward A. Teichert, Farrell Dobbs, Gerald L. K. Smith, John G. Scott, John Maxwell

1952
Dwight D. Eisenhower, president
Richard M. Nixon, vice president

Others supported: Adlai E. Stevenson, Vincent Halliman, Stuart Hamblen, Eric Hass, Darlington Hoopes, Douglas A. MacArthur, Farrell Dobbs, Henry B. Krajewski, Homer Tomlinson, Frederick C. Proehl, Ellen L. Jensen, Daniel J. Murphy

1956
Dwight D. Eisenhower, president
Richard M. Nixon, vice president

Others supported: Adlai E. Stevenson, Walter B. Jones, T. Coleman Andrews, Harry F. Byrd, Eric Hass, Enoch Arden Holtwick, William Ezra Jenner, Farrell Dobbs, Darlington Hoopes, Henry B. Krajewski, Gerald L. K. Smith, Homer Tomlinson, Herbert Shelton, Frederick C. Proehl, William Langer

1960
John F. Kennedy, president
Lyndon B. Johnson, vice president

Others supported: Richard M. Nixon, Harry F. Byrd, Orval Faubus, Eric Hass, Rutherford L. Decker, Farrell Dobbs, Charles Loten Sullivan, Joseph Bracken Lee, C. Benton Coiner, Lar Daly, Clennon King, Merritt Barton Curtis, Symon Gould, Whitney Hart Slocum, Homer Tomlinson, T. Coleman Andrews

1964
Lyndon B. Johnson, president
Hubert H. Humphrey vice president

Others supported: Barry M. Goldwater, Eric Hass, Clifton DeBerry, Earle Harold Munn, John Kaspar, Joseph B. Lightburn, Kirby Hensley, Homer Tomlinson, T. Coleman Andrews, Yette Bronstein, D. X. B. Schwartz, Louis E. Jaeckel

1968
Richard M. Nixon, president
Spiro Agnew, vice president

Others supported: Hubert H. Humphrey, George C. Wallace, Henning A. Blumen, Dick Gregory, Fred Halstead, Eldridge Cleaver, Eugene McCarthy, Earle Harold Munn, Charlene Mitchell

1972

Richard M. Nixon, president

Spiro Agnew, vice president

Others supported: George McGovern, John G. Schmitz, Linda Jenness, Benjamin Spock, Louis Fisher, Gus Hall, Harold Munn, John Hospers, John Mahalchik, Edward Wallace, Gabriel Green

On October 10, 1973, Spiro Agnew resigned as vice president. On August 8, 1974, Richard Nixon announced his resignation as president of the United States. After the resignation of Agnew, Gerald R. Ford was confirmed as vice president on December 6, 1973. He was elevated to the presidency on August 9, 1974, following Nixon's resignation. Nelson Rockefeller was nominated for the vice presidency on August 20, 1974, and began his term December 19, 1974. His appointment came as a result of Ford's succeeding to the presidency.

1976

Jimmy Carter, president

Walter Mondale, vice president

Others supported: Gerald R. Ford, Eugene McCarthy, Roger McBride, Lester G. Maddox, Thomas Anderson, Peter Camejo, Gus Hall, Margaret Wright, Lyndon H. LaRouche, Benjamin C. Bubar, Jules Levin, Frank P. Zeidler

1980

Ronald Reagan, president

George Bush, vice president

Others supported: Jimmy Carter, John Rarick, Edward Clark, John Anderson, David McReynolds, Clifford DeBerry, Gus Hall, Barry Commoner, Deidre Griswold

1984

Ronald Reagan, president

George Bush, vice president

Others supported: Walter Mondale, Gary Hart, Jesse Jackson, John Glenn, Alan Cranston, Reubin Askew, Ernest Hollings, George McGovern

Bibliography

American Glass from the Pages of Antiques: II Pressed and Cut. Princeton, New Jersey: Pyne Press, 1974.

American Heritage Auction of Americana Catalogue, Volumes I and II. New York: American Heritage Publishing Co., 1967.

American Heritage, Volume XIII, Number 5. New York: American Heritage Publishing Co., 1962.

Betts, John L., and Jack Allen. *History U.S.A.* New York: American Book Co., 1967.

Brown, Joseph G. *The Nation's Choice.* Milwaukee, Wisconsin: Association Corp., 1972.

Cloak, Evelyn Campbell. *Glass Paperweights of the Bergstrom Art Center.* New York: Crown Publishers, Inc., 1966.

Ferson, Regis F., and Mary F. Ferson. *Yesterday's Milk Glass Today.* Pittsburgh, Pennsylvania: Regis F. and Mary F. Ferson, 1981.

Freidel, Frank. *The Presidents of the United States of America.* Washington, D.C.: White House Historical Association, 1964.

Gores, Stan. *1876 Centennial Collectibles.* Fond du Lac, Wisconsin: Haber Printing Co., 1974.

Hake, Theodore L. *Political Buttons, Book II, 1920–1976, Political Buttons, Book III, 1789–1916.* York, Pennsylvania: Hakes Americana and Collectibles Press, 1977–1978.

Kahler, James G. *Hail to the Chief.* Princeton, New Jersey: The Pyne Press, 1972.

Kane, Joseph N. *Facts About the Presidents.* New York: Charter Communications, 1976.

Klamkin, Marian. *American Patriotic and Political China.* New York: Charles Scribner's Sons, 1973.

Kovel, Ralph, and Terry Kovel. *The Kovel's Complete Antiques Price List, Tenth Edition.* New York: Crown Publishers, Inc., 1977.

Marsh, Tracy. *American Story Recorded in Glass.* Minneapolis, Minnesota: Tracy Marsh, 1962.

McKearin, George P., and Helen McKearin. *American Glass.* New York: Crown Publishers, Inc., 1948.

Morgan, H. Wayne. *From Hayes to McKinley, National Party Politics 1877–1896.* Syracuse, New York: Syracuse University Press, 1969.

Newton, Charles B., and Edwin B. Treat. *Outline for Review American History.* New York: American Book Co., 1907.

Official Associated Press Almanac 1973. New York: Almanac Publishing Co., Inc., 1972.

Patterson, Jerry E. *A Collector's Guide to Relics and Memorabilia. New York: Crown Publishers, Inc., 1974.*

Peters, Harry T. *Currier and Ives, Printmakers to the American People.* Garden City: Doubleday, Doran and Co., Inc., 1942.

Peterson, Arthur G. *Glass Patents and Patterns.* DeBary, Florida: Dr. Arthur G. Peterson, 1973.

Presidency, Special Issue, American Heritage Volume XV, Number 5. New York: American Heritage Publishing Co., 1964.

Presidential Elections Since 1789. Second Edition, Washington, D.C.: Congressional Quarterly, Inc., 1979.

Ray, Marcia. *Collectible Ceramics.* New York: Crown Publishers, Inc., 1974.

Russell, Francis. *The Shadow of Blooming Grove.* New York: McGraw-Hill Book Co., 1968.

Smithsonian Institution. *Every Four Years.* Washington, D.C.: Smithsonian Exposition Books, 1980.

Stefano, Frank, Jr. *Pictorial Souvenirs and Commemoratives of North America.* New York: E. P. Dutton Co., Inc., 1976.

Stuart, Anna Maude. *Bread Plates and Platters.* Hillsborough, California: Anna Maude Stuart, 1965.

Sullivan, Edmund B. *Collecting Political Americana.* New York: Crown Publishers, Inc., 1980.

United States Presidents. Indianapolis, Indiana: The Curtis Publishing Co., 1980.

Warman E. G. *Antiques and Their Prices,* Fifteenth Edition. Uniontown, Pennsylvania: E. G. Warman Publishing Co., 1980.

Warner, Don. *Collection of Political Memorabilia Catalogue.* Boston, Massachusetts: New England Rare Coin Auctions, 1981.

Wearin, Otha D. *Political Americana.* Shenandoah, Iowa: World Publishing Co., 1967.

Index

About the Author

Presidential history and the mementos associated with our nation's leaders have fascinated author Stan Gores and his wife, Jeannine, for more than 20 years.

Not only have they assembled an outstanding collection, but, while he has been writing on the subject for magazines and newspapers, she has presented slide-lecture programs on presidential collectibles to clubs and antiques organizations.

His interest in researching the U.S. presidents while hunting for a wide variety of mementos led him to write the first edition of *Presidential and Campaign Memorabilia* in 1982. Now that book has been expanded into this comprehensive second edition.

A graduate of Northwestern University's Medill School of Journalism, Stan Gores also authored a book titled *1876 Centennial Collectibles and Price Guide* that sold out in two printings at the time the country was celebrating the Bicentennial. In addition, articles, columns, and stories he has written have appeared in three other books. Stan Gores also has written for such magazines as *Yankee, Ford Times, The Spinning Wheel, Hobbies, Antiques Journal* and the scholarly *Wisconsin Magazine of History;* and his byline has appeared in a number of newspapers, including the *Chicago Tribune, Milwaukee Journal, Detroit News* and the *Philadelphia Bulletin.* More than a half-dozen of his articles have been reprinted in the *Congressional Record.* His writing has earned him two National Freedom Foundation Awards along with awards from the Wisconsin Newspaper Association,

Wisconsin Association of School Boards, and the Wisconsin State Historical Society.

Mr. and Mrs. Gores live in Fond du Lac, Wisconsin where they have raised eight children and where he recently retired as managing editor of the *Reporter* newspaper.